The
Insanity Defense

By
Rudolph Joseph Gerber
Judge of the Superior Court of Arizona

ASSOCIATED FACULTY PRESS, INC.
Port Washington, N.Y. • New York City • London

Manufactured in the United States of America

Published by
Associated Faculty Press, Inc.
Port Washington, N.Y.

Library of Congress Cataloging in Publication Data

Gerber, Rudolph Joseph, 1938-
  The insanity defense.

  Includes index.
    1. Insanity—Jurisprudence—United States.
2. Criminal liability—United States.   3. Criminal
intent—United States.   4. Insanity—Jurisprudence—
Great Britain.   I. Title.
KF9242.G47   **1984**   345.73'04   83-15904
ISBN 0-86733-034-1   347.3054

Contents

Introduction 1

1. Early Tests for Insanity 7

2. Early Treatment Programs for the Insane 13

3. M'Naghten: The Man and the Test 21

4. Problems with the *M'Naghten* Rule 29

5. The Irresistible Impulse Test 37

6. The *Durham* Test 41

7. *Brawner:* The ALI Test 49

8. Insanity and *Mens Rea* 55

9. *Mens Rea* Cannot Be Abolished 63

10. Insanity as a Statutory Element and as an Excuse 71

11. Which Formulation of the Insanity Test Is Best? 77

Conclusion 91

Footnotes 93

Index 111

To
Jennifer and Kristin Gerber

Integer vitae scelerisque purus
non eget Maris jaculis...

Those with integrity and freedom
from crime do not need weapons of
war...

Horace, <u>Ode XXII</u>

Preface

This treatise has its genesis in the revision of the Arizona Criminal Code of 1978, when Arizona's territorial laws succumbed to a more modern statutory scheme. One of the topics which the Arizona legislature left untouched was the existing *M'Naghten* Rule for criminal insanity, which Arizona, like other states, inherited from the common law upon statehood. Since 1978, the confusion experienced by the Arizona legislature on this topic has been repeated in similar intensity in other state and federal law-making bodies. The recent acquittal of John Hinckley has intensified the lively academic debate of the past fifteen years and has given the topic more practical urgency, if not more clarity.

This extended essay represents yet another contribution to the "rivers of ink and forests of paper" devoted to a topic whose resolution, it seems, would be as unfavorable for the academic participants as it would be favorable for the law. In any event, the following pages reveal an attempt to take another look at the insanity defense from an interdisciplinary viewpoint, borrowing theories from historical, philosophical, legal, and medical schools of thought, with a final proposal on how the defense might be best retained while being revised.

Inspiration for the topic comes from those academic colleagues whose scholarly writings enliven the available moments of judicial reflection: Deans Norval Morris and Abraham Goldstein, Professors Paul Robinson, George Fletcher, and Herbert Packer, and many others. They share in the inspiration for, but not the shortcomings of, this further effort toward an understanding and modification of perhaps the most symbolically important feature of criminal law philosophy today.

R.J. Gerber

About the Author

Dr. Rudolph Gerber is a Judge of the Superior Court of the State of Arizona and a Professor of Business Law, Western International University. He holds the degrees of Bachelor and Masters of Art in Philosophy, Masters of Art in Comparative Literature, Doctor of Philosophy in Philosophy and a Doctor of Jurist in Law.

In addition to his legal experience in private practice and public offices he has received many scholastic and academic honors.

The most noted of these were the recipient of a Fullbright Fellowship at the Université de Louvain in Belgium and received a British University Scholarship to attend Oxford University.

INTRODUCTION

The chief cause of problems is solutions.

Eric Sevareid

Few issues preoccupy the arena of criminal law today as much as the fate of the insanity defense.[1] Some crime-conscious legislators in the spirit of the Nixon-Ford-Reagan administrations propose to inter the defense forever in order to curb its "unconscionable abuse."[2] Other reformers want to enlarge the categories of mental illness covered by the insanity defense so as to avoid supposedly unfair results, as for instance, when severe emotional trauma offers no mitigation for those incapable of perceiving right from wrong.[3] Other thinkers seek to eliminate the defense completely as the first step toward the entire abolition of mental elements from criminal law. Undoubtedly, the acquittal of John Hinckley in the attempted assassination of President Reagan will continue to fuel the fires of those advocating a restructuring of the defense.

The push-and-shove debates on the issue often resemble a legal taffy-pull as these groups become progressively entangled in a psychiatric-legal-moral morass. One writes now with an already gummy pen, in plain view of this looming morass. The only excuse for taking pen in hand again, short of delight in taffy for its own sake, is to make some suggestions that will avoid a further straitjacketing of criminal law energies.

At the heart of the debate lurk two focal issues: First, should the insanity defense be modified or abolished? Secondly, what is the impact of either on the supposition that a free will lies at the cornerstone of the criminal law? An aproach to these issues involves an investigation of the origin and history of the insanity defense, its various formulations, and the conflict between a free will versus a therapeutic concept of criminal responsibility. Of particular importance is an assessment of the advantages of the various existing tests for legal insanity, as well as the respective merits involved in the extremes of abolishing or widening the defense.

Undergirding all these issues lie basic philosophical problems rarely explored in the day-to-day transactions of the criminal law: first, whether there can be any reconciliation between the determinism of medical science and the free will postulate of the criminal law; secondly, whether *mens rea,* or "criminal intent," necessarily involves the postulates of freedom of the will and sanity; thirdly, whether the determination of sanity, and hence moral responsibility, is more properly a role for experts such as psychiatrists than for history's "twelve good men" of the jury.

The insanity defense is often interpreted to mean that legal responsibility can be ascribed only to one who possesses the ability to know and control his actions. It is considered unfair to blame and punish a person who lacks these capacities, which is the case with the mentally ill.

However, legal justification for an insanity test also raises the question about the *means* of determining insanity. Is there a scientific basis for differentiating between the sane and the insane? Are amoral people insane? There is no scientific evidence to demonstrate that the insane are less able to obey the law than the sane, although obedience may be harder for the latter. The cultural determinism issues thus raises this question: What is so unique about insanity that it alone should require an exception from criminal responsibility?

The traditional answer is that insanity involves some kind or kinds of medically definable mental illness analogous to a medically definable physical illness. But legal and the medical analyses obviously differ. While both seek to understand and control human behavior, the legal system approaches human behavior in terms of moral evaluation, whereas medical science approaches behavior in a scientific, value-neutral, empirical context. The legal model postulates that persons have free wills and are thus morally and legally answerable. By contrast, the scientific model is deterministic: Human behavior, like all phenomena, is caused by its antecedents, so that the concept of moral and legal responsibility becomes irrelevant if not archaic. From Darwin to

Freud to Skinner, the scientific method has implied that all human behavior can be explained in terms of cause and effect. That proposition undermines that comfortable generalization of the criminal law that people should be held accountable for their conduct.

The moral and legal basis for the special treatment of mentally disordered persons depends on two factual assumptions: (1) The insane are significantly different from most persons because they are ill; (2) Their legally relevant behavior is the product of their illness, not of their free, rational choice. Trust in these assumptions is the foundation of mental health law.

Unlike this legal model, the medical model sees *all* behavior as causally determined. Simplistically put, the medical model is deterministic: All phenomena, including behavior, are the effects of multiple interacting antecedent causes. Human thoughts, feelings, and actions are not the products of free will but the outcome of many biological, psychological, and social variables that have operated on the actor. Responsibility is thus scientifically irrelevant. When behavior can be perfectly predicted, the mythic notion of responsibility, as the Marxists once were tempted to predict, will "wither away."

Responsibility itself thus becomes a problem. Certainly it is true that the law says to the insane defendant: "You are not responsible for your acts because of your medical condition—what you have done is not your fault." Yet in treating the same individual, the psychiatrist often insists that the patient *must* accept responsibility for the consequences of actions. Thus the law rewards, and perhaps even encourages, irresponsibility while psychiatry attempts to discourage it.

Methods of determining responsibility or its absence have also varied. Until relatively recently the success of an insanity defense depended on how convincing a case could be made for neurological disturbances. Even in cases dominated by references to "delusions," "irresistible impulses," and other psychological conditions, the prevailing assumption was one of brain pathology, including forms of pathology originating in a defendant's lackluster pedigree. In only a small portion of these cases, however, was there ever proof of any kind of brain damage. The naturalistic tone of nineteenth-century thought expressed itself in the confident and unsupported belief that the mind was the shadow of the brain.

Today's ruling fad is environmentalism. As the expert of old was summoned to speculate on the condition of the defendant's brain or heredity or "humors," the contemporary court listens with reverent attention as psychiatrists and psychologists recount the woes of early neglect, antisocial behavior, poverty, and other sociological "determinants" of criminality. The medical model has been replaced by the psychosocial perspective, although the new view offers no more genuine expertise than the old. Courts like that involved with Hinckley learn that at the time the crime was committed, the defendant was "probably insane" or "probably sane"; that white males between twenty and thirty-five and of medium stature are the most likely to attempt a presidential assassination; and that television's celebration of violence creates a violent mental set in those already ravaged by societal neglect. The ultimate suggestion is that if we could only know all the sociological factors in a person's background, we could predict and control that person's behavior by eliminating these adverse conditions in the future. Crime is in the woodwork, not in the criminal.

Unfortunately, these supposed scientific approaches, whether sociological or medical, lack a solid scientific basis. The presence or absence of underlying disorders cannot always be demonstrated. The predisposing causes of deranged behavior are not any stronger than the predisposing causes of any other kind of behavior. There has been virtually no evidence of sufficient uncontrollable biological, psychological, or sociological causes of behavior.

In this vacuum, the legal system continues to flirt with the recurring medical dogma that disordered behavior is a symptom of an underlying, uncontrolled illness. This assumption implies that the actor is not the author responsible for disordered behavior any more than one is responsible for acquiring a fever or becoming blind. If all relevant human behavior is really the product of illness rather than of free choice, the legal system appears confronted with the total destruction of the free will postulate which is at the heart of criminal law.

Free will, thus, is a bone of contention between law and medical science. The criminal law still adheres to the premise that a person is able to choose freely and rationally. Psychiatry argues that we are not as free to choose as the law would believe.[4] A happy rapprochement between such views seems unlikely.[5]

The insanity defense thus lies squarely at the crossroads of legal and medical thought, with penal responsibility and scientific determinism at loggerheads. To add to the complexity, the protagonist of this very conflict remains mute since the insane person's motives are typically secret and inexplicable. Despite the advances of medical diagnosis and courtroom cross-examination, the motives for insane behavior remain an enigma. Indeed, it is an enigma which generates ironies. The more psychologically determined an act is, the more it appears inexplicable, and the more it is considered excusable. The very responsibility which psychiatrists deny in trial testimony is often urged upon the same patient as the key to successful treatment therapy.

The gap widens more sharply when law and medicine try to dictate each others' role in court. The mere presence of medical experts suggests domination and authority. Elite terminology and *hubris* at being cross-examined add to their air of infallibility. Psychiatric testimony implies that legal responsibility is a medical judgment inaccessible to, and incomprehensible by, lay jurors. The use of the behavioral medical model in court thus undermines the law's traditional adherence to the doctrine of personal responsibility and casts medical experts as father-confessors absolving guilt.[6]

Ultimately, one of the basic problems that has arisen over the past several decades of American criminal law has been the issue of the insanity defense and *mens rea* and their exclusion from the increasing determinism of this academic research. While the sociology of crime may be deterministic, and correctional theory also may be increasingly so, the criminal law's guilt-deciding process remains committed to a notion of personal responsibility developed long before the advent of the social sciences and medicine. The insanity defense has become a battlefield where these opposing ideologies face each other. Its symbolic importance for our jurisprudence outweights its practical significance in the courtroom.

Professional disagreement among medical experts also compounds the conflict. Trials involving an insanity defense are invitations to public cynicism about the objectivity of expert witnesses and of the court system itself. More often than not, the defendant admits his guilt but claims insanity as an excuse. Defense counsel presents expert witnesses preselected on the basis of their philosophical equation of criminal acts and mental illness. Prosecution experts typically are chosen on the basis of their rejection of this deterministic theory. Often these experts totally disagree with each other. While the public understands and accepts such disagreement, and at times sees the five-to-four decisions of the Supreme Court as illustrations of debate and independence, that same public tends to look with scorn on professional differences among medical experts, particularly in insanity trials. In short, since insanity is actually a legal rather than a medical concept, psychiatric disagreement is implicit in the issue, and the choice of expert medical witnesses by each side exploits that disagreement not only for the law and medicine but also for the public at large.

The answers to these kinds of dilemmas lie buried in interdisciplinary "gobblydegook." Law, moral philosophy, medical psychology, and sociology all make claims to expertise in this area. Specialists inevitably feel like strangers to concepts of mental disability imported from other disciplines. In consequence, legal reasoning in this area has often reflected either rigidity and parochialism, or, at the other extreme, a lack of confidence in its own inspiration reflected in overly generous hospitality to the latest fads in other specialties. In practice, a good part of the concern is the courts' continuing inability to recognize that an opinion does not become a fact merely because it is expressed by a doctor; to recognize that there can be no true expert testimony where there is no settled body of knowledge; and to recognize that laws are written because our impulses are often as strong as our judgment is clouded. The judiciary is too easily seduced by supposed experts, who in turn often are advocates of the petty battles of academe. Today each competing specialty casts the others as scapegoats: Psychiatry is unreliable and unscientific; law is archaic, moralistic, and punitive; sociology masquerades as science but is covert ideology; and moral philosophy is unrealistic, unscientific, and a play of linguistic acrobats. The history of this collaboration in court is one of "oscillation between simplistic optimism followed by chilling skepticism followed by a decade or so of silence and inaction with the cycle repeating."[7]

These and other perplexing issues, both theoretical and practical, lie at the heart of any effort to reform the insanity defense. It straddles the junction of law and medicine and of freedom and determinism. Its symbolic importance far outweights any of its specific formulations.

Chapter 1
Early Tests for Insanity

Make mad the guilty, and appall the free,
Confound the ignorant, and amaze indeed
The very faculties of eyes and ears.

Shakespeare, *Hamlet*

The Western philosophical tradition has given a prominent place to the doctrine of the duality of mind and body. Plato gave expression to this position when he differentiated the ideal world from the material world. The lawyer follows this philosophical tradition from afar in distinguishing between the criminal act and the mental element in crime. The mental element is referred to as intent or *mens rea;* the physical act is called *actus reus.* Both are necessary for the commission of a crime. Of the two require-ments, the *mens rea* or "guilty mind" ingredient has spawned controversy particularly as it relates to the insanity defense. As this chapter reveals, the history of both the *mens rea* and insanity concepts is interrelated—but not inseparably so.

Some writers such as J. Wigmore view primitive law as based on strict liability; that is, the actor's intent was not an element of the crime: "The doer of the deed was responsible whether he acted innocently or inadvertently, because he was the doer."[1] The act then is judged according to its consequence rather than in terms of its intent. On the other hand, Professor G.O.W. Mueller has argued that even in early primitive law, intention was an important aspect of the definition of both torts and crimes.[2] Mueller's position appears well-founded historically. The earliest expressed notion of legal responsibility appears in the Hebrew distinction between intentional and unintentional crimes. For the Hebrews, the archetypal examples of criminal incapacity were crimes committed by children and the insane, neither of whom was considered criminally responsible for these harmful acts.[3]

Later Greek philosophy and early Roman law recognized different kinds of motivation. The distinction between voluntary and involuntary wrongs was considered invalid by Plato because unjust acts were always done unwillingly. Plato conceded that calculated harms deserved more severe sanctions than those committed in passion. [4] More importantly, he invested human beings with "an element of free choice," which makes human beings, and not the gods, responsible for good and evil.[5] Responsibility and free will are thus closely allied in Plato.

For Aristotle, the distinction between voluntary and involuntary acts became more crucial. An act is voluntary, in his view, only when free from compulsion or ignorance. The capacity to choose is the "deliberate desire of things in our own power," the only determinant of culpability. Knowledge, not forethought, is the test of responsibility. A person is morally responsible if, knowing the circumstances and freed from external compulsion, he deliberately chooses to commit a specific act.[6]

Justinian's legal codification in the sixth century created a privileged legal status for children and the insane. A heat of passion test emerged. Justinian observed that punishment should be mitigated for a person who commits homicide "in a brawl."[7] The Venerable Bede, the English scholar, historian, and theologian, shortly thereafter concluded that children were incapable of "inner depravity" because they "will nothing of good or ill," though like madmen, they could make contracts.[8]

The *Dooms of Alfred*, which were probably promulgated during the ninth century, provided that "if a man be born dumb or deaf, so that he cannot acknowledge or confess his offenses," his father must pay his forfeitures. In the period between the ninth and thirteenth centuries, the same preferential treatment was extended to the insane, those who could not cooperate in their own defense, and those who were incompetent to stand trial.

This growing emphasis in the early Middle Ages on the mental state of the criminal was nurtured by two primary sources: an interest in the newly discovered Roman law, and the increasingly significant influence of the clergy on government policy.

During the twelfth century, the judges in the royal courts of England were primarily the clergy. The most notable instance of ecclesiastical influence was Henry de Bracton, whose *De Legibus et Consuetudinibus Angliae* (1300) borrowed heavily from early Roman law and strongly influenced the development of later English law. In 1264 Bracton became archdeacon of Barnstape and chancellor of Exeter Cathedral and in 1265 became chief judge of England's highest court, the Aulia Regis. Bracton was probably the first prominent medieval jurist to deal with the subject of insanity and crime. In the middle of the thirteenth century he wrote:

> For a crime is not committed unless the will to harm be present. Misdeeds are distinguished both by will and by intention (and theft is not committed without the thought of thieving). And then there is what can be said about the child and madman, for the one is protected by his innocence of design, the other by his misfortune of deed. In misdeeds we look to the will and not the outcome.

Bracton sought to avoid punishing those who lacked the requisite criminal intent to commit a crime. He consolidated the strict liability law of the courts with the element of moral intent urged by Church law. In his view it was the actor's intent which gave moral significance to the physical act and thus determined culpability.

In emerging from these philosophical and theological traditons, the early English common law did not at first recognize an insanity defense. Mental illness initially was not a trial defense but a tool for pardon. The Crown saw it as a reason to grant pardons to convicted murderers. In those days madmen were considered "akin to beasts" because they lacked full reasoning powers and were deprived of moral responsibility. This notion eventually bred the infamous "wild beast" test of insanity.[9] The "wilde beeste" test, as it is sometime spelled, is usually attributed to Bracton but, in fact, the concept apparently developed from the Aristotelian church psychology of the day which distinguished man from beast, which was mistranslated from Latin as "Brutus."[10]

By Edward I's reign (1272-1307), the concept of insanity as the "King's grace" entered the trial proper, where it usually functioned to mitigate punishment rather than guilt. As an excuse for criminal conduct it first appeared at the end of the reign of Henry III in the form of king's pardons granted to those judged insane.[11] These pardons were ultimately granted as a matter of course where sympathy dictated. Only the most dramatically infantile mental illnesses mitigated responsibility.[12] The criminal law of the period regularly perceived the insane person on the model of a young child in his moral and cognitive abilities.[13] According to the Elizabethan writer, Lambard, of Lincoln's Inn, writing in 1582:

> If a man or a naturall foole, or a lunatike in the time of his lunacie, or a childe y apparently hath no knowledge of good nor evil, do kil a ma, this is no felonious acte, nor any thing forfeited by it...for they cannot be said to have any understanding wil.[14]

Writing late in the sixteenth century, Lord Coke also compared the mental deficiencies of madmen with the mental capacity of children.[15] When Coke attempted to explain this standard to his Elizabethan contemporaries, he referred to a being so bereft of cognitive capacity as to have no greater competence than "an infant, a brute, or a wild beast."

For the better part of two centuries, a defendant whose crime revealed a coherent relation between motive and act had little chance of convincing a jury of his insanity. As Justice Tracy put it in the eighteenth century, not "every idle humor of man" could serve as grounds for exoneration. After Coke, Sir Matthew Hale, chief justice of the King's bench, noted that:

> An infant above fourteen and under twenty-one is subject to capital punishments, as well as others of full age; for it is *praesumptio juris,* that after fourteen years they are *doli capaces,* and can discern between good and evil.[16]

As for insanity, Hale stated that "such person as labouring under melancholy distempers hath yet ordinarly as great understanding as ordinarly a child of fourteen hath, is such a person as may be guilty of treason or felony." His definition of insanity rested on the "good and evil" test: The insane person is one who cannot distinguish good from evil. Hale distinguished two forms of insanity: partial and total. "Absolute madness," a total deprivation of reason, was a defense to a criminal charge because the accused could not have the required *animo felonico.* Such human beings were not persons but "brutes."[17] Partial insanity could function as a defense to a criminal charge only if contemporaneous with the act, a fact not easily provable.

In the pre-M'Naghten period, much of the contemporary insantiy defense had its roots in the the psychological concepts of phrenology, which left a lasting mark on the right and wrong test. Phrenologists believed that the human brain was divided into thirty-five separate areas, each with its own peculiar mental function. Hale himself adopts this rationale in speaking of the compartments of intelligence and will:

> The consent of the will is that which renders human actions either commendable or culpable...And because the liberty or choice of the will presupposeth an act of understanding to know the thing or action chosen by the will, it follows that where there is a total defect of the understanding, there is no free act of the will...[18]

Hale, however, explicitly recognizes the difficulty in devising rules for the practical application of his test: "For doubtless, most persons that are felons of themselves are under a degree of partial insanity when they commit these offenses."[19] He concludes that the division between the responsible and the irresponsible "must rest upon circumstances duly to be weighed and considered both by the judge and jury." In each case, the "best measure that I can think of" is whether or not the accused "hath yet ordinarily as great understanding as ordinarily a child of fourteen years hath."[20]

Hale's test did not gain wide use, possibly because an understanding of the relationship between age and mental capacity had not yet developed in scientific circles. Society at that time was unwilling to accept large-scale exoneration of criminals on the ground of insanity, seemingly because of no ready alternative to imprisonment. The requirement of total insanity embodied in the traditional "wilde beeste" test therefore continued to prevail.

Partial insanity disappears in the famous Arnold's case. Edward Arnold was convicted for having shot and wounded Lord Onslow while laboring under an insane delusion that Onslow had used imps to torture him. This case is usually referred to as the codification of the "wilde beeste" test of insanity in English common law. Yet the actual instruction to the jury does not really bear this out. In summing up the "wild beast" test to the jury, Justice Tracy used language precursory to M'Naghten's Test and in the process eliminated the defense of partial insanity:[21]

> If he was (in) the visitation of God, and could not distinguish between good and evil, and did not know what he did, though he committed the greatest offence, yet he could not be guilty of any offence against any law whatsoever;...a mad man...must be a man that is *totally* deprived of his understanding and memory, and doth not know what he is doing no more than an infant, than a brute, or a wild beast, such a one is never the object of punishment.... (Emphasis added)

Hadfield's case in 1800 added a more enlightened notion of the "wilde beeste" test as a basis for mitigating an admitted crime. James Hadfield had made an attempt on the life of George III, for which he was convicted of treason. His felony was set in motion by Bannister Truelock, who had convinced Hadfield that nothing less than the wishes of Jesus Christ Himself would be served by the death of the king. Hadfield's counsel, the future Lord Erskine, argued at trial that the defendant suffered from "motives irresistable" and from serious delusions. A person might think his neighbor a "potter's vessel," he argued, and proceed to do violence simply because such a delusion has disguised the victim's true nature. In Erskine's view, a person might know right from wrong, might understand the nature of the proposed act, and might even manifest clear design and foresight in planning and executing it, but if his mental condition caused the criminal act, the actor should not be held legally responsible. Erskine impressed the court with evidence of the head injuries suffered by Hadfield in his prior service to the king. In the end, the defense succeeded largely through the testimony of medical experts, who gave opinions that Hadfield's brain was severely impaired.

Later, in 1840, Edward Oxford attempted to assassinate Queen Victoria and Prince Albert.[22] Oxford was a victim of hereditary insanity; both his father and grandfather had been insane. The jury was told that Oxford's guilt or innocence depended on "whether he was under the influence of a diseased mind, and was really unconscious at the time." Like Hinckley, Oxford was eventually acquitted, much to the consternation of the royal family.

This pre-*M'Naghten* tradition reveals that insanity had no fixed medical definition, that it was invoked primarily to avoid capital punishment, and that it was more a factor in punishment than in deciding guilt. How its present role differs involves a complex evolution of law and medicine.

Chapter 2
Early Treatment Programs for the Insane

Hamlet denies it,
Who does it then? His madness—

Shakespeare, *Hamlet*

The checkered saga of the medical treatment of the insane begins in the early Middle Ages in an atmosphere of almost total neglect with occasional interludes of humane care.[1]

In the early thirteenth century, there existed in Gheel, Belgium, a precursor institution that cared for psychotic and retarded children and often arranged their adoption into compassionate families. St. Valentine's Hospital was built in 1486 at Alsace for the isolation and treatment of epileptics. The settlement of Moors in Andalusia contributed the first Spanish establishment for the mentally ill at Granada. The priory of St. Mary of Bethlehem in London, reconstituted as a mental hospital, was in full operation in 1547. In 1566 the Hospital of San Hipolito was established in Mexico by Bernardino Alvares, as the first institution devoted to the treatment of the mentally ill in the Western hemisphere.

Such treating establishments were the exception. The prevailing interpretation of insanity during the Middle Ages was witchcraft, that is, the insane were possessed by the devil. A sixteenth-century German physician named Johann Weyer first confronted this mentality with the observation that most witches were mentally or physically ill and that the monstrous acts inflicted on these sick individuals were unconscionable. Weyer's research sought to prove that witches were in fact only mentally ill and as such should be treated by physicians, not by clergy. He paid a price for his views. Weyer's contemporaries called him Weirus Hereticus or Weirus Insanus because his convictions deviated so "wierdly" from the attitudes of his day. Weyer even became the butt of legislation. The criminal code of Saxony, for example, contained the following editorial statement in 1572:

> In the course of the past few years many books have appeared in which sorcery is considered not a crime but a superstition and a melancholy, and these insist violently that it should not be punished by death. The *Wieri rationes* (Weyer's reasonings) are not very important, for he is a physician and not a jurist.

Jean Bodin, a French lawyer who defended the prosecution of witches, stated the legal views of the time:

> The judges cannot bring Satan into court, but they can diminish the scope of his power by taking from him those witches who help him, pray to him, pay obeisance to him, and carry out his instructions.

Apart from the institutions previously mentioned, special treatment for the insane during the early common law was virtually nonexistent. Indeed, the Middle Ages exhibited a staunch intolerance for any behavioral deviations, including those prompted by illness. The mad were regularly executed or thrown into gatehouses and prisons to furnish diversion for other prisoners. Those more fortunate were often driven out of the cities and abandoned to roam through forest and field as persons without a country. In northern Europe two unique modes of ritual exclusion developed: The mentally distracted were either crowded into "ships of fools" *(das Narrenschiff)* and shuttled from port to port, or were taken on pilgrimages to holy places and abandoned there for care by monks.

Where the Middle Ages tended to drive out the insane, the Renaissance sought to confine them. Some cloisters and monasteries were abandoned at that time, and the gradual abatement of leprosy resulted in vacating thousands of leprosariums. These vacated facilities provided convenient space for confining the mentally unfit.

Confinement enabled study and classification efforts. The best-known eighteenth-century proponent of a classification scheme for insanity was the Dutch physician Hermann Boerhaave (1668-1738). He accepted the notion of a relationship between illness and the four body humors. Melancholia, for example, was an illness caused by an excess of black bile. George Cheyne (1671-1743) suggested that neurotic behavior was common in England, pointing out that no less than he himself, a Fellow of the College of Physicians, was a serious neurotic. Anyone at all could suffer from emotional problems, he argued, and there was no need to be humiliated by it. His book, published in 1733, was entitled *The English Malady: Or a Treatise of Nervous Diseases of All Kinds, as Spleen, Vapours, Lowness of Spirits, Hypochondriacal and Distempers.*

Robert Whytt (1714-1766) divided the neuroses into hysteria, hypochondriasis, and nervous exhaustion ("neurasthenia"). He theorized that disturbed movements within the nervous system produced nervous problems. Of all these schemes, probably the most comprehensive classification of mental illness was proposed by William Cullen (1712-1790). He was the first to use the term *neurosis* to refer to illnesses not related to local pathology or fever. He proposed a fourfold classification of the neuroses: *Comata* (apoplexy, stroke); *Adynamiae* (changes in the autonomic nervous system); *Spasmi* (disturbance of voluntary muscles, for instance, convulsions), and *Vesaniae* (intellectual impairment). Cullen's therapeutic approaches were a mix of science and speculation: exercise, physiotherapy, diet, cold dousings, blistering of the forehead, purging, bloodletting, and vomiting.

Giovanni Battista Morgagni, an Italian physician, after investigating eight hundred autopsies, published in 1761 *De sedibus et causis moborum per anatomen indagatis* ("On the Seats and Causes of Disease Investigated by Anatomy"). Morgagni believed that illnesses were related to specific organs. He argued that the symptoms caused by a stroke were not due to brain pathology per se, but to broken blood vessels that affected the brain. As a result of Morgagni's work, other neurologists, neuroanatomists, and physicians interested in mental illness attempted to localize these diseases in the brain.

Philippe Pinel (1745-1826), physician, teacher, philosopher, and reformer, also proposed his preferred classification system. As physician-in-chief at Bicetre and La Salpetriere, and on the basis of observations made on his patients, Pinel categorized the psychoses into melancholias, manias without delirium, manias with delirium, and dementia (idiocy and intellectual deterioration). He

differentiated among problems of attention, memory, and judgment and recognized the importance of the emotions in causing
mental illness. Mental disorders, he thought, might possibly be
due to a lesion in the central nervous system.

The treatment of mental illness by the medical establishment
did not lead automatically to more humane techniques. During
the Enlightenment Bethlehem lived up to its linguistic corruption
as "Bedlam." Its conditions were filthy, the food abominable, and
the treatment brutal. Regular therapy consisted of emetics, purga-
tives, bloodletting, and torture. Bedlam became a favorite holiday
outing for Londoners. Even as late as 1815 the institution exhibited lunatics to the public for a penny every Sunday. Despite its
advances over England, France was hardly more humane.
Anyone could visit the Bicetre for a guided tour, and during such
tours, attendants would flick their whips ands make the mad
dance and do acrobatics to amuse the visitors. In the "Lunatics
Tower" in Vienna, first built in 1784, the inmates were placed in
the spaces between the outer and inner walls, where they could
be observed from within by their captors, and from below by
people passing by on the streets. Mental institutions of the era
toyed with the notion that the insane were spectacles both for
delight and for insight into their psychic secrets.

Major improvements occurred at the time of the French Revolu-
tion. Jean Baptiste Pussin, later known as the governor of the
insane, who served both at Bicetre and at La Salpetriere, released
the patients from their chains, opened their windows, provided
them with nourishing food, and generally treated them with
compassion. Revolutionary France implicitly felt that such treatment was appropriate, if only because so many healthy revolu-
tionaries, in their own way, had just emerged from bondage and
intended to bring freedom to others who were enchained.

Pinel's successor at Salpetriere, J.E.D. Esquirol (1772-1840) attempted to revise the laws in order to further protect the mentally
ill. Pinel's successor at Bicetre was Guillaume Ferrus (1784-1861).
His interests eventually resulted in the French law of June 30,
1828 requiring more humane treatment of the insane which
became a model for other European countries. During the reign of
Louis Philippe, a revised French penal code established even
more liberal views of insanity, particularly as a mitigation of
criminal guilt. Witchcraft was on its way out in western Europe.

The leavening influences of the Renaissance and of the Refor-
mation also bore fruit in the various Germanic states. Various new
penal codes reflected multiple conditions which could affect a

person's criminal mind. For example, the Bavarian Code of 1813, followed by that of Saxe-Weimar in 1838, provided that no punishment should be imposed on the following exhaustive classes of persons: children under eight years of age; insane persons, idiots, persons who had lost their judgment from either melancholy or from other mental afflictions; those who could not judge the consequences of their actions or were not aware that a penalty was attached to such actions; those who by reason of weakness caused by old age had lost the use of judgment; deaf and dumb persons; those who were of incurable ignorance; and finally, those who had committed a crime while in a confused state of mind. A broader sympathy for human weakness is difficult to imagine. The code even appears to have been administered with Germanic precision.

England remained largely aloof from thse Continental reforms in treating the insance. The majority of English mental patients prior to the *M'Naghten* case were paupers. As late as 1844 many of these patients were turned over without examination to workhouses that operated under the jurisdiction of the Poor Laws. There they were kept in degrading and inadequate quarters. Particularly in England, phrenology was accepted as the reigning medical science. According to that medical theory, the human mind was compartmentalized into thirty-five chambers, each with a corresponding mental function; for example, the sixth area, "Destructiveness," was found above the *ear meatus*. One part of the mind could thus become disordered while the rest remained normal. Thus the medicine of the day propagated a view now considered erroneous.

America remained even more aloof than England from Continental reforms although some progress was made. Benjamin Rush of Pennsylvania (1745-1813) became the first American physician to teach a course on mental disease, which he felt was due to an excess of blood in the brain. Accordingly, in his practice he drew great quantities of blood, even up to six quarts over a period of a few months. His patients naturally became much less agitated as their strength declined, leading Rush to assume that their condition had improved. Rush also believed that many insane people could be cured by being properly frightened. One of his favorite techniques was to convince the patient that death was imminent. He also devised a gyrating chair that would whirl about his ill patients, thereby loosening congealed blood in the affected brain.

Before 1810 only a few Eastern seaboard states had established institutions for the mentally ill. Only Virginia had established a public asylum. The insane commonly languished in local jails or poorhouses or lived with family and friends. New York and Massachusetts erected mental institutions in the early 1830s, as did the agricultural states of the Eastern seabord by the late 1830s. These exceptions notwithstanding, the common American view of mental illness still contained a strong alloy of witchcraft and possession.

From this selective historical tour of the asylum prior to 1843, several conclusions emerge. First, mental patients were treated harshly for at least two reasons: They were often considered witches and/or possessed by the Devil. In any event, they were silent and inexpressive. No one saw their black humors, their "animal spirits," and no one could discover the physical seat of their disturbances. The insane generated fear precisely because they kept their motives and designs buried from public inspection, to the consternation not only of witchcraft-minded clergy, but also of probing doctors and judges.

One also notes throughout this history the overwhelming correlation between insanity and phrenology, with the one counterpointing the other. Recurring analogies to children and to "wild beasts" reflect the notion that the insane person's deprivation of free will supposedly flowed from the disease of the will's counterpart, the intellect. In the Aristotelian faculty psychology of the day, eventually reinforced by the English jurist and philosopher, Jeremy Bentham the intellect appeared as the regal psychic faculty grasping the moral nature of the proposed act. The intellect then presented the act for adoption or rejection by its sister faculty, the will, which in turn sought approbation from yet another compartment, the emotions. Each mode of control was ancillary to rational comprehension. Totally impaired cognition could easily recommend a distorted course of conduct to the will and a consequent distortion in emotional reaction. The opposite, however, was lightly dismissed: It was not thought possible in this theory for a distorted emotional scheme or volitional choice to distort cognition. Insanity thus spread "downward," not "upward."

Not surprisingly, this historical development reveals a corresponding common-law ambivalence over partial versus total insanity. Lying at the heart of this honest confusion as to which should excuse are at least two important but ill-defined insights of emerging medicine: First, sanity is not an absolute, fixed state but a fluctuating condition existing on a continuum with insanity. This conclusion was supported by the observation that "wild beasts" and children at times did appear to grasp the fact that their criminal deeds were criminal. Awareness of evil, like awareness of morality generally, was possibly subject to days of insight and days of darkness. Sanity was perhaps a matter of degree, not a constant possession. Secondly, this history of treatment efforts records the policy, crystalized for a time in the thirteenth century, that insanity should be a factor in the determination not of guilt but of pardon. Insanity evidence thus was oriented to considerations such as treatment and punishment, particularly to avoiding capital punishment.

In sum, this history reveals that the law of insanity throughout Europe and America followed rather than led the medicine of insanity. Most of the codes based on the Napoleonic model incorporated the notion that mental disorders are incompatible with legal responsibility. Most of these codes also incorporated the older notions of *dementia* and *furor* from the existing medical knowledge of insanity. Neither the leading theoreticians like the Italian jurist and economist, Cesare Beccaria and Bentham, nor the code draftpersons elaborated upon these traditional notions nor sought new relationships between punishment and criminal medicine, except to affirm generally that penal justice must cure the leading social illness, crime itself. Thus it was not from "above," from legislatures, but rather from "below," from trial processes and medical laboratories, that psychiatric medicine eventually entered and modified the law of insanity.

These historical and theoretical developments set the stage for the famous *M'Naghten* case of 1843.

Chapter 3
M'Naghten:
The Man and the Test

I seen my opportunities and I took 'em.
George Washington Plunkett of Tammany Hall
circa 1900

Much of the modern insanity defense in the Anglo-American world derives from a bizarre English trial in 1843. Daniel M'Naghten, a wood turner in Glasgow, suffered from delusions of persecution: He felt that Sir Robert Peel, the British prime minister, the Jesuits, and the Pope, were all conspiring against him. Unable to get at the Jesuits or the Pope, he came to London with the intention of assassinating the chief of government. His plan would have succeeded but for the fact that Peel chose to ride in Queen Victoria's carriage because of her absence from the city, while Drummond, his secretary, rode in the carriage normally occupied by Peel. Believing that the prime minister was riding in his own carriage, M'Naghten shot and killed Drummond. In the quaint legalese of the day, M'Naghten was thereafter charged with first-degree murder of Drummond, who "lanquished, and lanquishing, did die."

His trial[1] developed into a battle between medical knowledge and ancient legal authority.[2] In anticipation of the insanity defense, the prosecutor opened the case with a learned discussion of the background of criminal insanity. Nine medical witnesses testified for the defense that M'Naghten was totally insane. The defense relied in large part on Dr. Isaac Ray's scholarly *Medical*

Jurisprudence of Insanity, published in 1838.

Ray's treatise contained contemporary medical views on the weakness of the current right-wrong test. Ray conceded at the outset the difficulty of differentiating abnormal from ordinary behavior and in particular between behaviors caused by personality differences. The author found no fault in permitting a jury of laypeople, rather than experts, to settle the question. Nonetheless, Ray offered some useful guidelines. One should be wary of associating only the most outlandish behavior with disease, and one should also extend rather than limit the possible symptoms. Madness, he wrote, is not indicated by any particular extravagance of thought or feeling. A patient could be quiet and insane or noisy and sane or degrees of both. An insane person also could reach logical conclusions but not moral ones and could also make correct moral decisions in an illogical way. Insanity thus was a very broad condition; it could show up in cognitive matters or in moods such as melancholia or *dementia* or simply in violent conduct.

Ray's treatise was quoted along these lines at length to the *M'Naghten* jury. The *M'Naghten* defense used by Ray proposed a medical model of responsibility to replace the existing legal test based on the moral ability to distinguish right from wrong. The *M'Naghten* jury was told that the human mind is not compartmentalized and that a defect in one aspect of the personality could easily affect other areas.

The court was so impressed with medical evidence concerning M'Naghten's incompetency that Lord Chief Justice Tindal practically directed a verdict for the accused. "...I cannot help remarking," he commented to the jury, "that the whole of the medical evidence is on one side, and that there is no part of it which leaves any doubt in the mind."[3] Instead of directing a verdict (as his words effectively did), he committed the case to the jurors who found the defendant not guilty on the ground of insanity.[4] M'Naghten was committed to Broadmoor, a mental institution, where he later died.

After M'Naghten's trial, both Houses of Parliament and Queen Victoria expressed concern about whether M'Naghten's acquittal presaged a dangerously liberalized state of affairs in the criminal law.[5] The establishment's reaction to M'Naghten's acquittal appears in the address of the lord chancellor to the House of Lords:

> A gentleman in the prime of life of a most amiable character, incapable of giving offence or of injuring any individual, was

murdered in the streets of this metropolis in open day. The assassin was secure; he was committed for trial; that trial has taken place, and he has escaped with impunity. Your Lordships will not be surprised that these circumstances have created a deep feeling in the public mind, and that many persons should, upon the first impression, be disposed to think that there is some great defect in the laws of the country with reference to this subject which calls for a revision of those laws in order that a repetition of such outrage may be prevented.[6]

The trial also came under written attack. Editorials from the *Illustrated London News* argued that M'Naghten was only simulating insanity and that softheaded judges and doctors had let him escape justice. It was even suggested that Bedlam, the "Eden of St. George's Fields," was a soft and pleasant place. A second editorial reiterated the same concepts, and stated that Bedlam was a "retreat of idleness" and that perhaps M'Naghten and other criminals were "profitably insane." Immediate curative legislation was suggested.

Queen Victoria herself wrote a letter to Peel expressing her dissatisfaction with the administration of the insanity defense:

Buckingham Palace, 12th March, 1843. The Queen returns the paper of the Lord Chancellor's to Sir Robert Peel with her best thanks.

The law may be perfect, but how is it that when ever a case for its application arises, it proves to be of no avail? We have seen the trials of Oxford and MacNaghten (sic) conducted by the ablest lawyers of the day—Lord Denman, Chief Justice Tindale, and Sir Wm. Follett—and *they allow* and *advise* the Jury to pronounce the verdict of *Not Guilty* on account of *Insanity*—whilst *verybody* is morally *convinced* that both malefactors were perfectly conscious and aware of what they did! It appears from this, that the force of the law is entirely put into the judge's hands, and that it depends merely upon his charge whether the law is to be applied or not. Could not the Legislature lay down that rule which the Lord Chancellor does in his paper, and which Chief Justice Mansfield did in the case of Bellingham; and why could not the judges be *bound* to interpret the law in *this* and *no other* sense in their charges to the Juries?

Actually, M'Naghten's exculpation helped the Tory government minimize the considerable political problems then plaguing it. M'Naghten himself made a statement to the court which bore out his own hatred of the Tories:

> The Tories in my native cities have compelled me to do this. They follow and persecute me wherever I go, and have entirely destroyed my peace of mind...I cannot sleep at night in consequence of the course they pursue toward me ...They have accused me of crimes of which I am not guilty; they do everything in their power to harass and persecute me; in fact, they wish to murder me.[7]

In any event, the queen asked the House of Lords to "take the opinion of the judges on the law governing such cases." Consequently, the fifteen judges of the common law courts were called in extraordinary session under subtle pressure to answer five complex questions on the status of criminal responsibility in England. Lord Chief Justice Tindal, responding for fourteen of the fifteen judges, articulated what has come to be known as the *M'Naghten* "Rule" or "Test." Tindal wrote:

> Your Lordships are pleased to inquire of us, secondly: "What are the proper questions to be submitted to the jury, where a person alleged to be afflicted with insane delusion respecting one or more particular subjects or persons, is charged with the commission of a crime (murder, for example), and insanity is set up as a defence?" And, thirdly: "In what terms ought the question to be left to the jury as to the prisoner's state of mind at the time when the act was committed?" And as these two questions appear to us to be more conveniently answered together, we have to submit our opinion to be, that the jury ought to be told in all cases that every man is to be presumed to be sane, and to possess a sufficient degree of reason to be responsible for his crimes, until the contrary be proved, that, at the time of the committing of the act, *the party accused was labouring under such a defect of reason, from disease of the mind, as not to know the nature and quality of the act he was doing, or if he did know it, that he did not know he was doing what was wrong.* The mode of putting the latter part of the question to the jury on these occasions has generally been whether the accused at the time of doing the act knew the differences between right

and wrong; which mode, though rarely, if ever, leading to any mistake with the jury, is not, as we conceive, so accurate when put with reference to the party's knowledge of right and wrong in respect to the very act with which he is charged. If the question were to be put as to the knowledge of the accused, solely and exclusively with reference to the law of the land, it might tend to confound the jury by inducing them to believe that an actual knowledge of the law of the land was essential in order to lead to a conviction; whereas the law is administered upon the principle that every one must be taken conclusively to know it. If the accused was conscious that the act was at the same time contrary to the law of the land, he is punishable; and the usual course, therefore, has been to leave the question to the jury, whether the party accused had a sufficient degree of reason to know that he was doing an act that was wrong; and this course we think is correct, accompanied with such observations and explanations as the circumstances of each particular case may require.[8]

The judge's response was only an advisory opinion, "a hotch-potch of the law as laid down from the time of Bracton."[9] Nonetheless, it influenced the law for nearly the entire English-speaking world since his day. As Professor H. Wingo and others have observed,[10] the M'Naghten Test solidified in its day the repeated earlier attempts to settle British legal thinking on the troublesome insanity issue and formally established the defense as a legal excuse. In response to Ray's attempt to substitute a medical model for a legal one, the English judges sought to establish new legal criteria for what they considered a legal rather than a purely medical problem. The new test was thought to give an accurate legal criterion for distinguishing those who were responsible and punishable from the irresponsibles needing hospitalization.

M'Naghten's unequivocal recognition of the "right and wrong" standard as an established rule and the national attention it attracted at the time made it a case of special significance. With its sharp focus on the offender's ability to know right from wrong with respect to the particular act charged, the M'Naghten Test clarified and organized confusing precedents and produced a distinct, workable rule for its day from which more modern tests for insanity have evolved.

The new rule's balance sheet, however, is far from exclusively positive. Rather than relying on the medical insights of Dr. Ray's monumental work, Tindal, with the queen's heavy breath upon him, reaffirmed the old right-wrong test despite the fact that it echoed such uninformed concepts as phrenology and monomania and froze the notion of mental compartmentalization in the law just when that concept was becoming medically obsolete. Dr. Ray's medical insights were thus lost to the common law for over a hundred years.

The *M'Naghten* Test and its ensuing evidenciary rules also accorded privileged status to psychiatrists as experts and prophets in the still-infant field of mental disease. For centuries lunacy had been treated as a condition discernible to the naked eye. That concept changed when insane delusion became recognized as a form of insanity. Delusions come and go; they are invisible. They do not cause frenzy, foaming, or convulsions. Insanity thus ceased to be a matter of common discernment and required medical experts or "alienists" to separate the sane and the insane. Doctors could offer an expert opinion concerning an event which neither they nor anyone else actually witnessed but which they alone could reconstruct with newly developed medical hypotheses not subject to objective verification. While they still could not determine the objective fact of insanity, the new test permitted them to testify whether the accused had been suffering from a disabling disease at the time of the offense and to state whether the criminal act was a product of that disease. The *M'Naghten* Test thus planted the seeds for psychiatric posturing in the courtroom and for the reduction of legal responsibility to a medical issue—exactly what Ray's treatise desired and what the English judges sought to avoid.

Even in its own day, *M'Naghten's* contemporaries began to question the wisdom of a rule developed by fiat rather than via the case-by-case method traditional with English common-law. Mr. Justice Maule, the fifteenth member of the panel summoned by the House of Lords, concurred in the formulation of the test but expressed reservations about answering questions put to the judges abstractly without benefit of a particular case. The noted legal historian, Sir James Stephen, observed that every insanity judgment delivered since the year 1843 was founded on an authority which "deserves to be described as in many ways doubtful." Dr. Henry Maudslay, Isaac Ray's contemporary, remarked shortly after the adoption of the *M'Naghten* Test that its authors were adhering to an absurd position discredited by medical science.

Indeed, within several years after *M'Naghten,* its medical foundations did change. Within the discipline of psychiatry, the theory of monomania was abandoned shortly before 1870, at least for two reasons: First, because the notion of a partial insanity bearing only on one part of the mind was replaced by the notion that mental illness could affect not simply the "mind," but also noncognitive functions such as emotions and instinct, and could do so while leaving thought patterns intact; secondly, because of the development of the notion of inherited mental degeneration affecting differing persons of a family at differing periods in their own individual lives or in their family tree.

These and other shortcomings of the *M'Naghten* Test deserve fuller elaboration.

Chapter 4

Problems With
the <u>M'Naghten</u> Rule

[The *M'Naghten* Rule]...stands almost immutable; it is the impenetrable wall behind which sits entrenched the almost unconquerable prosecutor; it is the monster of the earnest psychiatrist which prevents him from introducing into the courtroom true understanding of human psychology and the psychology of the criminal act.

Gregory Zilboorg, M.D., (1954)

\ The *M'Naghten* Rule was seized upon avidly by the courts of the British Isles, excepting Scotland, and by the then existing states of the United States except New Hampshire. In the ensuing century, despite advances made by psychiatry, the *M'Naghten* Rule remained substantially unchanged. It continues today to color most of the trials of the criminally insane in the courts embracing the Anglican legal system. It remains the sole test of criminal responsibility in approximately one third of the states. In some states the rule is supplemented and broadened by the irresistible impulse test. Courts in some of the jurisdictions which adhere to *M'Naghten* have expressed dissatisfaction with the rule but refuse to discard it on the ground that such a change must come from the legislature. In any event, the rule remains and continues to exert both a real and a symbolic message about criminal responsibility and its relationship to knowledge.

The ways in which the *M'Naghten* Rules have been applied vary in practice in the countries which still retain them.[1] After an exploration of British data, Nigel Walker concludes that while a strict interpretation was generally upheld at appeal, juries often seemed to disregard them if the offender's mental condition aroused their sympathy. Professor Walker notes similar anomalies in Australia's experience. However, Goldstein and Marcus argue that U.S. courts have often been prepared to accept a broader definition, and they criticise both lawyers and psychiatrists for not exploiting this.

The *M'Naghten* formula is filled with paradoxes. Not the least of these is that its own moral and cognitional criteria should have convicted rather than acquitted its namesake, whose planning and concealment reveal his awareness of the wrongfulness of his act.

Under the *M'Naghten* Rule, the accused is not criminally responsible if a mental disease at the time of the act prevented him from knowing the nature and quality of the act or that it was wrong.[2] The basic postulate of the test is the capacity to follow the right course once one is able to perceive it.[3]

This emphasis on cognition reflects a rationalist era. At the time of *M'Naghten,* cognition was seen as the highest function of the personality. Philosophers searching the Cartesian dregs of the period expressed the notion that the mind controlled bodily behavior like an angel driving a machine. The rule assumes that if an individual "knows" right from wrong, his rational powers are intact and that he is, therefore, capable of governing his conduct.

This view has been largely rejected in psychology. The theory of partial insanity or monomania, that is, that a person could be sane in all other respects and yet have a cognitive delusion, has also been exploded by the more modern theory of the integrated psyche. Psychologists are diverse as Freud, Jung, Carl Rogers, and Skinner now maintain that cognition is not the sole or even the principal controlling function of the psyche. Volition, impulse, the subconscious, or the environment may each at times overpower control and/or cognition. The psyche is now seen as integrated rather than compartmentalized, as "openness to experience," rather than as narrowly cognitive.

By contrast, the emphasis in *M'Naghten* is on the cognitive capacity to understand the moral nature of acts.[4] The rule assumes that when cognition is defective, the personality as a whole is so impaired that the accused cannot grasp the wrongfulness of his actions.[5]

The objects of knowledge differ in the two branches of the test. The first branch is satisfied by a description; the other requires an evaluation. The first question is whether an accused had suffi- cient ability to appreciate the nature and quality of his act and evokes a description of his deliberations. Describing the nature and quality of the act specifies what is meant by the psychiatrist's "reality principle," that is, knowledge of actions and their every- day consequences. The second branch of the test assumes that an accused knew the nature and quality of his act and asks whether he had the capacity to appreciate that the act was wrong. This standard requires an evaluative statement, not a description of the context of the act.[6]

Two other phrases of the *M'Naghten* Test cause major trouble: The terms *disease of the mind* and *know*. Courts have not precisely defined *disease of the mind*, but this phrase clearly is not equivalent to all the various medical classifications of mental disease. Taking its meaning from the rest of the test, the phrase becomes limited by the word *know*. To qualify as a "disease of the mind," a malady must touch an accused's reflective powers so severely that the actor is deprived of any knowledge of the nature and quality of his act, so that he does not know that what he was doing was wrong. Noncognitive mental disorders are, therefore, not "diseases of the mind."[7] Few of the psychoses and severe forms of other mental disorders literally come within the framework of "disease of the mind." The word *know*, however, becomes ambiguous for patients suffering from serious mental illness not directly cognitional. A sick person's knowledge is often divorced from all affect, somewhat like the knowledge that child- ren have of mimetic propositions they recite without understand- ing.

The required knowledge crucial for legal responsibility is an appreciation or awareness of legal and moral consequences, not an abstract assent to a proposition. A fundamental difference exists between verbal or intellectual knowledge, on the one hand, and knowledge so fused with affect that it is humanly appreciated.[8] Since everyday understanding is not confined to abstract intellectual processes like geometry, the word *know* in the *M'Naghten* Test lacks the practical sense of affect. The cogni- tion in question is totally different from purely intellectual assent to a moral proposition.[9] As the Royal Commission on Capital Punishment stated in 1953:

...(T)he *M'Naghten* Test is based on an entirely obsolete and

> misleading conception of the nature of insanity, since insanity does not only, or primarily, affect the cognitive or intellectual faculties, but affects the whole personality of the patient, including both the will and the emotions. An insane person may, therefore, often know the nature and quality of is act and that it is wrong and forbidden by law, but yet commit it as a result of the mental disease.[10]

Many of the objections to the *M'Naghten* formulation reside in the view that it reflects a minimalistic policy regarding the entire class of irresponsible people; that is, it fails to adequately identify all those mentally disabled persons who may deserve to be excused from criminal responsibility. The test calls for total impairment: the accused must not know *at all.* This traditional English hallmark of "total" insanity continues to require a near impossibility. Few, if any, persons are total madmen; insanity is rather a matter of degree. *M'Naghten's* single-track emphasis on the cognitive aspect of the personality recognizes no degrees. The defendant either knows right from wrong or does not; that is the only choice the jury is given. In fact, however, our mental institutions, as any qualified psychiatrist will attest, are filled with people who to some varying degrees do differentiate between right and wrong, but lack the constant capacity to control their acts.

The law needs to acknowledge differing shades of gray rather than the absolutes of sanity versus insanity. The existing rigidity accords with neither the facts of mental illness nor the demands of legal, ethical, or social policies. Mental illness rarely if ever destroys the cognitive awareness required by the test; it may, however, destroy, in part, the capacity to use such knowledge to control behavior. Because the *M'Naghten* Test focuses only on the cognitive aspect of the personality, that is, on the ability to know right from wrong, it does not permit a jury to identify those who can distinguish between good and evil but who cannot control their behavior. This observation reflects the difficulty psychiatrists describe in giving expert testimony under the *M'Naghten* formulation. The test requires a total impairment of cognitive capacity whereas psychiatric experience reveals only a graded scale.

A further defect of the *M'Naghten* Rule stems from its legalistic shackle—and halo—placed on experts. Since the law limits a testifying psychiatrist to stating his opinion as to whether the accused is capable of knowing right from wrong, the expert is compelled to test guilt or innocence by a concept which bears little relationship to current psychiatric realities. He necessarily considers the mind as a logic-tight compartment in which the delusion holds sway with the balance of the mind intact.

Prominent psychiatrists have expressed their frustration when confronted with such patchwork requirements. Echoing such complaints, some psychiatrists ask, "How (does one) translate 'psychosis' or 'psychopathy' or 'dementia praecox' or even 'socio-pathy' or 'mental disorder' or 'neurotic character disorder' or 'mental illness' into a psychiatric judgment of whether the ac-cused knows 'right' from 'wrong'?" In stronger terms, Dr. Law-rence Kolb, former director of the New York Psychiatric Institute, professor and chairman of the Department of Psychiatry at Co-lumbia University and director of the Psychiatric Service at Presb-yterian Hospital, has declared that "answers supplied by psychia-trists in regard to questions of rightness or wrongness of an act or 'knowing' its nature constitute a professional perjury." Whether a psychiatrist is capable of determining the existence of an individu-al's capacity to make ethical judgments has been seriously questioned.[11] One eminent psychiatric authority has said,

> To force a psychiatrist to talk in terms of the ability to distinguish between right and wrong and of legal responsibil-ity is...to force him to violate the oath he takes as a witness to tell the truth and nothing but the truth.[12]

Dr. Bernard Diamond has observed that if the psychiatrist is to be truthful on the witness stand, he must say that,

> Just about every defendant, no matter how mentally ill, no matter how advanced his psychosis, knows the difference between right and wrong in the literal sense of the phrase—(thus the psychiatrist) becomes an expeditor to the gallows or the gas chamber.[13]

Since psychiatrists normally utilize other criteria apart from a defect in cognition to detemine responsibility, the *M'Naghten* language widens the chasm between legal and medical insanity. Psychiatrists are forced to make wholly personal judgments about the guilt of the defendant, and juries are forced to choose bewtween the extremes of guilt or insanity without any middle ground.[14] The result is that the insanity determination ceases to be a legal, communal decision and becomes instead an arbitrary medical judgment with more caprice and more extremism than a lay decision would produce.

The foregoing analysis echoes a redundant and widely accept-ed criticism of the *M'Naghten* Rule. The test, however, has re-ceived major rehabilitative surgery at the deft hands of Dean Abraham Goldstein. In *The Insanity Defense* (1967 and 1982) he argues that the verbal limitations of the test in practice are really no bar to courtroom admission of broad psychiatric evidence, including evidence going well beyond cognitional defects. Hence the restrictive *M'Naghten* language in practice is harmlessly inop-erative.

Goldstein's observations are well-founded as to evidentiary practice in the courtroom. Few if any *M'Naghten* jurisdictions restrict admission of psychiatric evidence strictly to cognitional defects. Much "loose" psychiatric evidence *is* received in court. The test shows its restrictive colors, however, when judges or juries must weigh the admitted evidence on the *M'Naghten* scale. In the typical case, a jury immersed in a mass of psychiatric data uses the restrictive *M'Naghten* jury instruction as a winnowing device for separating wheat from chaff. In this sifting process, the decisive and solitary factor becomes a cognitional defect, for that is the instruction given the jury, indeed usually taken into the jury room.

The evidence-instruction dilemma reflects the widespread cour-troom practice of freely admitting far more evidence than strictly permitted by the test, under a libertarian feeling that any such evidence ought to be heard, and then instructing the jury under strict *M'Naghten* guidelines to disregard most of it. This practice effectively brands the admitted, noncognitional evidence irrele-vant to the determination of insanity. Since the insanity instruc-tion should mirror the test, the instruction cannot be altered without altering the test, which itself cannot be remedied by simply opening the evidentiary floodgates.

There lingers another murky, linguistic issue which Dean Gold-stein similarly minimizes. Insane persons clearly *do* know; they *do* intend their acts. A paradigm of many examples, M'Naghten himself manifestly intended a killing, carefully premeditated it, and knew it to be wrong and punishable. This is precisely what his lengthy deliberation and his careful concealment of his plans connote. A strictly honest reading of his test on its face would exonerate neither M'Naghten nor many, if any, similarly insane defendants. To this problem, it is adequate to reply, as do Gold-stein and others, that the cognitional and moral language of the test requires a "commendably broad" interpretation, that the test should mean "fully" or "really appreciate one's behavior." These suggestions amount to admitting that the test not only does not mean what it says but also that it will exculpate nearly everyone. Thus a dilemma: The exact language of the test would literally convict nearly all insane persons; its liberal interpretation ("really appreciate") would acquit nearly all sane persons, none of whom "really" or "fully" appreciate all the moral implications of behavior.

Ultimately, however, it is not likely that juries will lightly accept the notion that a person who seemingly knew in a true sense did not "really" know in a legal sense. One would expect jury skepticism; indeed, the system is healthier for it. The true vice of M'Naghten, therefore, is not that psychiatrists feel constrained to give artificial testimony but rather than the ultimate decision-makers are required to ignore extracognitional evidence vital to their final judgment of insanity.

Whatever the social climate of Victorian England, today's introspective society is not as satisfied with a rigid notion of mental illness defined exclusively in terms of the inability to know. In this setting, a test which depends on psychiatric notions already discredited when adopted no longer represents an enlightened view of criminal responsibility.

Chapter 5
The Irresistible Impulse Test

Make mad the guilty and appall the free,
Confound the ignorant and amaze, indeed,
the very faculties of eyes and ears.

Shakespeare, *Hamlet*

As has been shown, the most widely accepted criticism of *M'Naghten* is that it deals only with the capacity for understanding. It equates criminal responsibility with moral cognition and thereby limits the excuse of insanity to persons with defective cognition. A defense of insanity based on noncognitive conditions existed in England even before the *M'Naghten* Test but was ill-defined and seemingly ill-considered. The possibility of a non-copgnitive mode of insanity was not mentioned by the justices in drafting *M'Naghten*, for their ruling interpretation of all insanity was that exemplifed by M'Naghten himself, namely, insane delusions. During the latter half of the nineteenth century, however, some American jurisdictions began to experiment with an irresistible-impulse appendage to the right-wrong test to address claims of insanity based on defects in psychic processes other than cognition.

↯ Today the irresistible-impulse test, a frequent companion to *M'Naghten*, is nowhere relied on as the sole criterion of criminal responsibility. It has been entirely rejected in England, Canada, and some twenty-two states, but in at least fifteen states, it is accepted in conjunction with the *M'Naghten* Test, thus liberalizing the range of criminal responsibility. This test applies to a defend-ant who may know the nature and quality of is act and who may be aware that it is wrong, but who, nevertheless, is irresistibly driven to a criminal act by an overpowering impulse resulting from a mental condition. The rule may have had its genesis in 1834 in Ohio.[1] First applied in Alabama in *Parsons* v. *State* in 1887, this test judges a person to be insane if he satisfies the *M'Naghten* Test or "if, by reason of the duress of such mental disease (the actor has) so far lost the power to choose between the right and wrong,...as that his free agency was at the time destroyed..." Five states have adopted this combined test.[2]

The test language is typically put by New Mexico's Supreme Court:

> Assuming defendant's knowledge of the nature and quality of his act and his knowledge that the act is wrong, if, by reason of disease of the mind, defendant has been deprived of or has lost the power of his will which would enable him to prevent himself from doing the act, he cannot be found guilty.[3]

The test represents the first wholesale amendment of, or addi-tion to, *M'Naghten*. Text writers have misnamed this the irresisti-ble-impulse test, but it is really a control test. Dean Goldstein has found so many differing formulations of the test that he concludes that "there is no monolith called the irresistible-impulse test."[4] Their universal thrust, however, is a loss of control, and their universal motivation is to remedy *M'Naghten*'s omission of non-cognitive control evidence.

The Irresistible-impulse test language has problems at least as great as those in the *M'Naghten* Rule. Weighty objections are raised by the notion of a sudden, impulsive or irresistible loss of control. Just as the intellectual interpretation of the *M'Naghten* knowledge requirement ignores emotional factors, the "sudden impulse" emphasis in the control test restricts evidence and jury deliberations solely to emotional immediacy,[5] thus keeping from the jury the durational aspect of an accused's mental condition. [6]

The "impulse" connotation also fails to account for cases where a loss of volition takes place not suddenly but gradually,[7] as in cases of melancholia and paranoia. While giving consideration to the defendant's capacity to control his actions, the test also implies a "sudden and immediate gratification of an urge," where temporary postponement is generally possible.[8] The test gives no consideration to the defendant whose mental disease shows brooding, introspection, and excessive reflection. The language of "control" suggests that an individual with sufficient powers temporarily to control or forestall impulses is legally sane even though completely dominated by these impulses. If the capacity for temporary control exists, the jury may reason that the impulse was not actually irresistible.

The irresistible-impulse standard thus becomes an arbitrary juggling of definitions rather than an assessment of real behavior. Only the most obvious forms of a loss of control receive consideration, whereas more subtle but just as compelling behavioral problems are virtually ignored.[9] In effect, the irresistible-impulse test, like all its variant control tests, gives no criteria for distinguishing an impulse which *could not* be resisted from one which merely *was not* resisted in fact.

Whether or not an "irresistible impulse" can exist in a person able to distinguish right from wrong is not a question to be decided by judicial fiat. The view that certain impulses which result from mental disorders may be irresistible has formidable medical support. Although the problem of proving the existence of such an impulse is difficult, it may be no more difficult than proving the capacity to know right from wrong.

The irresistible-impulse test has also been criticized even by those who agree with its basic attempt to take willpower into account. Criticism is directed at the misleading interpretation of the test as implicitly restricted to sudden spontaneous acts as distinguished from insane propulsions accompanied by brooding or reflection. "Irresistible impulse" implies a total impairment of volitional capacity, yet medical science asserts that impulses which are absolutely impossible to resist are rare occurrences, especially in the commission of serious crimes.

To this critique, Goldstein and others again rejoin that the definitional defects in the test are irrelevant since, once again, the restrictive impulse language of the test rarely excludes any kind of psychiatric evidence in the courtroom.[10] The real problem once again, however, is that the evidentiary "strainer" is not as determinative of the outcome as is the jury's (or court's) deliberative "scalpel"—that is, reliance on the jury instruction helps the jury hack a pathway through the psychiatric jungle. Jury instructions using the impulse-language effectively tell the jury to filter out, or at least to minimize, noncognitional, nonimpulsive psychiatric data, with the result that the mentally sick who are neither impulsive nor moronic are found sane. The problem becomes more acute in view of the fact that the mentally ill seldom commit their crimes at the height of their psychic disorganization (since depression immobilizes) but only after the psychotic impulse has passed away. Jury instructions do not recognize this possibility.

Ultimately, the irressistible-impulse test is more a legal than a medical miscreation. If the psyche is indeed integrated, the concept of a will separate from cognition is untenable. Furthermore, there are no symptoms that, in and of themselves, are always ungovernable or uncontrollable. Coupled with the fact that most mental illness is not impulsive in its manifestation, these defects raise doubt about the continued utility of the irresistible-impulse test used either alone or in conjunction with the *M'Naghten* Rule.

Chapter 6
The <u>Durham</u> Test

"The judge is the expert of experts" should be turned around; it is up to the expert to be the judge of judges.

Michel Foucault

In 1954, the Court of Appeals for the District of Columbia reversed the conviction of Monte Durham for housebreaking and petit larceny.[1] The court held that *Durham* had presented enough evidence on the question of insanity to raise an issue regarding the District of Columbia's version of the *M'Naghten* Test.[2] In the course of a long opinion, the court rejected the *M'Naghten* Rule in all its formulations for a "broader test" of insanity: "[A]n accused is not criminally responsible if his unlawful act was the product of a mental disease or mental defect."[3]

Some members of the psychiatric profession saw *Durham* as a response to long-standing demands for a more humanitarian test. Articles in psychiatric and legal journals praised the new test as a long-awaited enlightenment. Indeed, some of the praise seemed excessive. Karl Menninger acclaimed the *Durham* Rule as "more revolutionary in its total effect than the Supreme Court decision regarding segregation." Judge David Bazelon, its author, was awarded a certificate of commendation by the American Psychiatric Association. Some legal comments praised it as "careful and psychologically literate."[4] Judge Learned Hand, on the other hand, commented that "it did not seem to me to give us any guidance that perceptibility would help."[5] Other psychiatric commentary ranged from "unadulterated nonsense,"[6] to "both psychiatry and jurisprudence ought to be grateful for the enlightened courage of the three judges who were responsible for the new turn in our criminal jurisprudence."[7]

If one theme pervaded Judge Bazelon's opinion, it was to encourage the fullest possible range of psychiatric evidence on the issue of criminal responsibility. Instead of restricting testimony, *Durham* intended to encourage the psychiatrist, "[w]hatever the state of psychiatry," to present the court and jury with all possible information to answer the question, "Why did this defendant do these things?" Bazelon himself composed an explanatory set of instructions to psychiatric experts to accompany orders for mental examinations. These instructions were to be read aloud in court before the first expert testified. They read, in part, as follows:

> As an expert witness, you may, if you wish, and if you feel you can, give ;your opinion about whether the defendant suffered from a mental disease or defect. You may then explain how the defendant's disease or defect relates to his alleged offense, that is, how the development, adaptation, and functioning of the defendant's behavioral processes may have influenced his conduct. This explanation should be so complete that the jury will have a basis for an informed judgment on whether the alleged crime was a "product" of his mental disease or defect. But it will not be necessary for you to express an opinion on whether the alleged crime was a "product" of a mental disease or defect and y ou will not be asked to do so.
>
> What is desired in the courtroom is the kind of opinion you would give to a family which brought one of its members to your clinic and asked for your diagnosis of his mental condition and a description of how his condition would be likely to influence his conduct. Insofar as counsel's questions permit you should testify in this manner.

The inquiry might include, but was not to be limited to, the traditional test. After all the evidence had been presented, the jury would then apply this ultimate standard:

[The] accused is not criminally responsible if his unlawful act was the product of mental disease or mental defect…The question will be simply whether the accused acted because of a mental disorder, and not whether he displayed particular symptoms which medical science has long recognized do not necessarily, or even typically, accompany even the most serious mental disorder.

Despite Bazelon's instructions, the *Durham* opinion left undefined the key term *mental disease or defect*. Early cases under *Durham* showed little concern with the missing definition. Lawyers and judges turned to the psychiatrists, who responded that a psychosis was a mental disease (or a "mental disorder") and that anything else was not.[8]

One major issue was whether the term *mental disease* was to be limited to psychotic conditions, as was characteristic of previous tests, or expanded to include neuroses, personality disorders, and other minor disorders such as mucous colitis, tension headaches, and neurodermatitis. The *Durham* Test seemed initially to represent a scientific advance in criminal jurisprudence. Actually, it represented the psychiatrization of the criminal law, the transformation into legalese of the medical notion that there are two right modes of behavior—one sane, the other insane. The *Durham* standard viewed mental functioning as essentially unitary but multifaced. In fact, however, no single mental faculty determines the existence or nonexistence of sanity, just as no single faculty is responsible for the control of human behavior. Impaired control may result from a wide variety of causes in the psyche, not all of which are cognitional.

Durham thus created its own ambiguities. While its language permitted the psychiatrist to testify on the full range of rational, emotional, and volitional elements influencing an individual's psyche, the test drew an inflexible line between criminal responsibility and acquittal. The test gave no place for the psychic reality of a fluctuating or graduated scale of responsibility.[9] This absolute distinction between the responsible and the nonresponsible is generally unacceptable to modern psychiatry, which views an individual as responsible, if at all, only to the extent that the person is free to control action. In this view, freedom is a floating variable, not a fixed state. Psychiatrists prefer to say that a person's freedom is present, if at all, in inverse proportion to his neuroticism; in other words, the more his acts are determined by a malevolent consciousness, the less free he is. The psyche thus manifests degrees of freedom and degrees of responsibility.[10]

Defining "mental disease" in *Durham* rapidly became an acute problem. Under *Durham*, the term *mental disease* became synomous with psychosis, with the apparent agreement of most trial participants. Psychiatrists then thought they were using a legal term with an understood legal meaning; lawyers believed they were using a medical term with a standard medical content. The definitional problem erupted in 1957, when the staff of Saint Elizabeth's Hospital decided that nonpsychotic diagnoses, particularly the diagnosis of "sociopathic personality disturbances," would be explicitly recorded in reports of mental examinations, thus opening the insanity defense to a larger number of defendants.

Because most indigent defendants in the District of Columbia were examined at Saint Elizabeth's, the psychiatrists there played a major role in shaping the actual manner in which the *Durham* Rule was administered. Saint Elizabeth's psychiatrists began to testify in court that personality disorders were, indeed, "mental diseases." The number of acquittals by reason of insanity rose dramatically: In the four years following *Durham* (1954-57), there had been 34 such acquittals; in the four years following the change in policy (1958-61), there were 150, and in 1961 and 1962, the acquittal rate was running at 66 per year. (See Table A in footnote 11.) The increase seemingly came not at the cost of a decrease in the conviction rate but at the expense of adjudications for incompetence, followed by the dismissal of the criminal charges. Professor Reid has remarked that "what seemed to be emerging under the *Durham* rule was that neither legal principles nor medical concepts determined the defendant's fate so much as did administrative label changing by the hospital's staff."[11]

In view of the pro-psychiatric orientation of the *Durham* Rule, and given the fervent approbation with which the psychiatric community originally greeted *Durham*, the attitude of Saint Elizabeth's psychiatrists toward the daily use of the test became ironic. After an intensive investigation of the operation of the rule R. Arens concluded:

> An assay of public psychiatric facilities in the District of Columbia, undertaken by the project, alongside of the study of the attitudes manifested by trial judges and juries, found the psychiatric opposition to an expanding insanity defense no whit less than that of the psychiatrically unsophisticated public. Psychiatric attitudes, particularly those encountered

at Saint Elizabeth's Hospital, were marked by massive fears of the breakdown of the already scarce resources of the public hospital and by the unexpectedly punitive orientation of public psychiatrists.[12]

Arens reported that one psychiatrist, when asked to explain the discrepancy between his own view that an offender was mentally ill and his testimony in court that the offender was not ill, said:

> Sure, the man is sick. Under the *Carter* case, moreover, I would say that his crime is the product of mental illness. But I choose to accept a stricter legal standard because if I did not, we would be flooded with undesirables, who are not acutely ill and who would clutter up our facilities which are already strained to the breaking point.[13]

Ultimately at least four intertwined problems arose with the vague "mental disease" language employed by *Durham*. In the first place, the test failed to define the parameters of mental disease clearly enough to determine whether sociopathy would count. Durham himself was diagnosed a sociopath and held sane. Shortly thereafter, one Blocker, on trial for murdering his wife, pled insanity, was diagnosed a sociopath, and also found guilty. One month later, however, when the St. Elizabeth's staff began to broaden its forensic concept of mental disease to include sociopathy, Blocker appealed and was granted a new trial. This sudden reversal of psychiatric opinion on the legal process provoked judicial tempers. Judge Warren Burger, now chief justice of the Supreme Court, angrily stated:

> The terms [now] mean in any given case whatever the expert witnesses say they mean...No rule of law can possibly be sound or workable which is dependent upon the terms of another discipline whose members are in profound disagreement about what those terms mean...We tacitly conceded the power of Saint Elizabeth's Hospital staff to alter drastically the scope of a rule of law by a "weekend" change in nomenclature which was without any scientific basis.[14]

The innuendo was clear: Saint Elizabeth's had changed its labels to bring a greater number of defendants under the protective umbrella. Neither legal principles nor medical concepts would determine the defendant's fate as much as label-changing by the hospital's staff.

This first problem brought a second: the domination of the courtroom by psychiatrists. Whereas Judge Bazelon had hoped to open the door to unrestricted psychiatric testimony, in fact he opened the floodgates to medical conjectures frequently both inscrutable and overbearing. Particularly onerous to the jury's role was the tendency by psychiatrists to voice unfounded statements regarding the vexing issue of which psychic conditions did or did not cause the criminal act, thus permitting psychiatrists to determine the ultimate legal issue of criminal responsibility.

Most psychiatrists responded to *Durham* by providing a conclusory diagnosis, providing opinions on the ultimate issue without reasons to support that conclusion. Bazelon lamented that *Durham* was supposed "to open the inquiry to the widest possible scope of medical testimony," but in case after case the result was to "narrow the inquiry rigidly to the magic words *disease* and *product*."[15]

The issue became acute in testimony regarding the "productivity" requirement. The central question became: How does the jury determine whether an act was the "product" of a mental condition? Should the psychiatrist testify that it was, or was not? Is this a psychiatric question for the expert witness, or is it a factual-moral question for the jury? For the years of *Durham's* tenure, the courtroom practice was for the psychiatrists to testify on this issue, even after the circuit court had prohibited the practice. The recalcitrance of those charged with the responsibility for effectively administering or faithfully following *Durham* thus became a major factor in its demise.

Judge Bazelon became progressively less enchanted with psychiatrists in the courtroom. In *Rollerson* v. *United States,* he warned: "The frequent failure to adequately explain and support expert psychiatric opinion threatens the administration of the insanity defense in the District of Columbia."[16]

Thirdly, the *Durham* Test sparked a philosophical debate reflecting the problems of free will that have always beset the insanity defense. As Judge Bazelon viewed the product test, his perspective was that of a person versed in the knowledge of psychodynamics and inclined toward the theory of psychic determinism. His colleague, Judge Burger, relied on the traditional rationalist arguments from Aristotle through Bentham to the effect that humans chose freely. The Bazelon test was for Burger a denial of free will. Bazelon's positions gradually withered away in subsequent decisions as sociopathy disappeared as a mental disease under *Durham*.

Finally, and more crucially, the *Durham* Rule focused on mental illness, not mental state, as the crucial factor. While other tests such as *M'Naghten* focus on an incapacitating condition resulting from mental illness or defect, *Durham*, in leaping directly from mental illness to act, ignored causes of incapacitation apart from mental illness. The test also was more concerned with mental illness than with *mens rea*. *Durham* implied that mental illness itself, not the state of mind arising from mental illness, was the excusing factor. Such a rule could not be a valid test of responsibility unless *all* mental illnesses became conditions impairing the volitional or cognitive processes of the defendant.[17]

Durham's demise was desultory; it left behind a mixed legacy. It was even blamed for increasing crime rates in the District of Columbia. In an effort to curb this high rate of crime, the House District Subcommittee recommended legislation to reestablish the right-and-wrong test in the District of Columbia and to require "substantial evidence" before the insanity issue could be raised as a defense. The resistance to *Durham* was also witnessed in Congress as a whole, which promptly passed a mandatory commitment statute so that offenders acquitted by reason of insanity would be automatically committed to a mental hospital without any further mental investigation.

Despite the initial enthusiasm which *Durham* generated, it was adopted only in Maine and the Virgin Islands.[18] It has been specifically rejected in nearly thirty jurisdictions, including all the federal circuits. Although it lived a life of only thirty years, it generated a wealth of insanity jurisprudence unrivaled elsewhere. Chief Justice Burger, then a member of the District of Columbia Circuit, remarked that in its brief span, a body of case law developed that would have taken fifty years to grow elsewhere. In those years, that court explored legal issues never raised in other jurisdictions.

Ultimately, the major flaw in *Durham* resides in its identification of the moral issue of responsibility with the scientific issues of diagnosis and causation. Bazelon's personal goal appears, in part, to have been to turn the court trial into a morality play with psychiatrists as the actors. Other judges administering *Durham* also discovered that psychiatric affirmation of the medical facts of disease and causation unduly influenced the jury on the suppressed issue of value; that is, whether the accused was to be morally blamed for the crime. The conversion of these neutral medical issues into legal and moral issues exceeded the competence of the psychiatric experts and judges who achieved it. In the end *Durham* failed because moral and legal guilt was reduced to a purely medical question. More specifically, psychiatry failed the courts because it could not deal with the prospect of criminal behavior caused simply by a mind which was evil rather than sick.

Chapter 7
Brawner: The ALI Test

Insanity is often the logic of an accurate mind overtaxed.

O. W. Holmes

In the major 1972 case of *United States* v. *Brawner*,[1] the influential District of Columbia Court formally abandoned the *Durham* Test and opted for a variant of the American Law Institute's (ALI) insanity proposal. Chief Judge Bazelon, the author of *Durham*, wrote a separate opinion emphasizing his agreement that *Durham* should be retired in favor of the ALI Test. He disagreed with almost everything else in the majority opinion.

The facts in *Brawner* were simple. Brawner's jaw had been broken in a fight. He returned half an hour later with a gun, and fired five shots through a closed apartment door killing one of the occupants. Four expert witnesses agreed that Brawner was suffering from a psychiatric or neurological abnormality, variously described as an "epileptic personality disorder" or a "personality disorder associated with epilepsy." The government witnesses apparently regarded Brawner's actions as a legitimate response in light of his severe injury. As one of the doctors testified, "I think I would, too, under the same circumstances, want to get even with somebody who broke my jaw." Brawner nonetheless was convicted.

Determined to abandon Durham, the *Brawner* court turned to the ALI's proposed rule of criminal responsibility:[2]

1. A person is not responsible for criminal conduct if at the time of such conduct as a result of mental disease or defect he lacks substantial capacity either to appreciate the criminality (wrongfulness) of his conduct or to conform his conduct to the requirements of law.

2. As used in this Article, the terms *mental disease or defect* do not include an abnormality manifested only by repeated criminal or otherwise antisocial conduct.

The court intended that this new rule would lessen the influence of expert testimony encouraged by *Durham*. Seemingly less stultified and less likely to create a mystique for expert testimony, the ALI language of "result" and "substantial capacity" presumably would result in better communication among experts, judges, and juries.[3] Feeling that the "product" language of *Durham* led to its downfall, the *Brawner* court specially endorsed the "as a result of" language, stressing only that some general causal relationship was a necessary element of any insanity defense. The "substantial capacity" requirement sought to correct the long-standing reference in earlier cases to the need for total impairment. To include emotional trauma within the rule, the court adopted language whereby the defendant "appreciates the wrongfulness of his conduct," rather than the version focusing upon the "criminality" of his conduct. The court held that the caveat in paragraph 2 should be available to a judge as a rule of application but not for inclusion in instructions to the jury.[5] Evidence of past criminal and antisocial actions that would demonstrate mental disease would be inadmissible unless accompanied by expert testimony.

More importantly, the *Brawner* opinion dispensed with two alternative proposals for handling insanity. Aboliton of the defense was considered a legislative rather than a judicial prerogative.[6] The court also rejected Judge Bazelon's suggestion that the jury be instructed that a defendant lacks criminal responsibility "if mental disease impairs his capacity or controls to such an extent that he cannot justly be held responsible."[7] The court felt that such a free-wheeling rule—or non-rule—would encourage subjective notions of sympathy and prejudice to color jury determinations.[8]

In retrospect, despite its superficial aplomb, the *Brawner* opinion reveals serious inconsistencies touching on the relationship between the insanity defense and *mens rea*. The *Brawner* court's jury instruction on insanity stated: "You are not to consider this defense unless you have first found that the government has proved beyond a reasonable doubt each essential element of the offense."[9] This instruction on its face means that insanity becomes an issue only after prior determinations that the defendant (1) did the criminal act, and (2) did so with its defining mental element; that is, intentionally, knowingly, and recklessly. The insanity defense comes alive, then, only for defendants already inculpated in crime and possessing a criminal *mens rea*. As an issue subsequent to *mens rea*, the insanity defense is therefore not an evidentiary standard for weighing intent or free will at all but an escape valve for persons whose guilty mental state is disturbed beyond the limits of legal responsibility.

Having once established this distinction between *mens rea* and the insanity defense, the *Brawner* opinion erases that distinction completely in stating that it refuses to abolish the insanity defense because its abolition would eliminate free will from the criminal law.[10] The court could reach this conclusion only by confusing the proposal to abolish the insanity defense with the much more sweeping proposal to abolish *mens rea*. It further mistakenly assumes that the abolition of insanity would inaugurate strict liability crimes; that is, criminality apart from criminal intent, when, in fact, such a result follows only from the abolition of *mens rea*.[11] These assumptions are inconsistent with the court's own suggested jury instruction. They contribute nothing toward clarifying the relationship of insanity and *mens rea*.

The legal issue in *Brawner* was neither *mens rea* nor the abolition of the insanity defense; the concern simply was the propriety of the *Durham* Test. In rejecting *Durham*, the *Brawner* court wandered into alien pastures and became lost in a dark forest of foreign issues. While *Brawner*'s abolition of *Durham* is a plus factor, the rest of the opinion only increases the confusion on the larger issues of what *mens rea* and insanity are for and how they interrelate. The decision more than fulfills Judge Bazelon's comment: "While the generals are designing an inspiring new insignia for the standard, the battle is being lost in the trenches."[12]

The ALI Test itself is not without linguistic difficulty even apart from its ties to the *Brawner* decision. The addition of "defect" to disease broadens the test to include the retarded, whose conditions might not be regarded as either a "disease" or an illness.

Unlike *M'Naghten,* the *Brawner* Test omits a specific reference to "defect of reason." Professor H. Fingarette regards this omission in the ALI Test as "fatally vague...and potentially misleading because it can be taken to imply that what is ultimately at issue is involuntariness or ignorance, whereas what actually ought to be at issue is irrationality."[13]

The ALI Rule also emphasizes that "any" incapacity is insufficient to avoid criminal responsibility but that "total" incapacity is also unnecessary. The ALI drafters intended to incorporate in their rule a volitional element that would avoid the "total impairment" notion appended in some states to the irresistible impulse test. In their view, the irresistible impulse test required a complete impairment of the capacity for self-control, a criterion that poses great difficulty to psychiatrists. To the ALI drafters, the disorientation of the schizophrenic is rarely total because most psychotics have some capacity to conform to a norm. It is not entirely clear, however, what the drafters meant by the word *substantial.* On one hand, they spoke of avoiding "total" impairment. They also spoke of an impairment reflecting "the most severe afflictions of the mind."[14] In *Wade* v. *United States,* 426 F.2d 64 (9th Cir. 1970), a seven-to-six decision adopting the ALI Rule, five judges joined the dissenting view of J. Trask, who wrote:

> The modifying word *(substantial)* creates more problems than it solves. The explanation is so mystical that it approaches the supernatural. How is the jury to know what *substantial* means? How does anyone know except the user?...The jury could believe that a twenty-five percent lack of capacity is *substantial* and acquit one who is otherwise morally responsible.

The phrase *conformity of conduct to the requirements of law* represents a distinctive change from the *M'Naghten* Rule. Professor Fingarette calls the test in this respect "misleading" because it

> apparently calls for speculation about whether there has been a literal breakdown of invisible, inner mental control machinery such that the person could not do otherwise than he did. But typically the insane person could have done otherwise if he had elected otherwise... Unless we engage in unverifiable metaphysical speculations about "breakdowns of the will," we must see that typically there is every evidence that the criminally insane person had both the

physical and mental capacity to perform a law-conforming act rather than a law-transgressing act. What he lacks is the mental capacity to elect rationally which act to perform.[15]

Professor Jerome Hall has argued that the "incapacity to conform (one's) conduct to the requirements of law" allows a defendant to rest his defense entirely on the independent and autonomous alternative of "irresistible impulse," the change being merely one of expression, not one of substance. Hence Hall believes the ALI Test is worth only as much as the "irresistible-impulse" test and vulnerable to the same criticisms previously leveled at that test.[16] On the other hand, Judge J. Biggs states that the phrase *conform his conduct to the requirements of law* is "substantially the same rule of responsibility as that laid down by the *Durham* case,...though the reporters...in their comments expressly repudiate the doctrine of the *Durham* decision.[17]

The second paragraph of the *Brawner*-ALI formulation "is designed to exclude from the concept of 'mental disease or defect' the case of so-called psychopathic personality."[18] Judge Biggs expresses the opinion that since there is doubt as to whether the psychopathic personality constitutes a valid psychiatric classification, no rigid exclusionary rule should be attempted.[19] One medical commentator[20] questions the validity of equating the "psychopathic personality" with repetitious "criminal or otherwise antisocial conduct," since it is doubtful that any psychiatrist would rest a finding of psychopathy only on a history of repeated criminal or otherwise antisocial conduct. The exclusion of the psychopathic personality by the Model Penal Code is "tantamount to the usurpation of the functions of the psychiatrists in helping to formulate realistic legislation." One major objection to the *Durham* Rule was precisely the opposite: *Durham* would include the class of sociopaths.

In retrospect, the *Brawner*-ALI Test, nearly now universal in the federal circuits, broadens the inquiry beyond the cognitive limitations of *M'Naghten* and the strictly causal confines of *Durham*. The new test conforms generally to the definitions of insanity used in Germany since 1871 and codified as well in the Soviet Union.[21] These tests consist of the following elements:

1. A definition of relevant categories of mental illness[22]
2. A statement linking the mental illness to a particular deficiency in the execution of the criminal act
3. A definition of two types of deficiency in the execution of

the crime, a cognitive deficiency, and a volitional one[23]

In sum, the ALI Insanity Test developed in *Brawner* and now adopted in nearly all federal circuits extends the defense beyond cognitive defect to include volition as well. It raises seemingly unresolvable problems with the notions of "substantial capacity" and "result of." Insofar as it touches on volition and motivation, the new test leaves with its followers at least two tenacious substantive issues regarding the relationship between insanity and free will on the one hand, and between insanity and *mens rea* on the other. Both issues deserve careful elaboration.

Chapter 8
Insanity and <u>Mens Rea</u>

Experience should teach us to be most on guard to protect liberty when the government's purposes are beneficient.

Mr. Justice Brandies,
dissenting in *Olmstead* v. *U.S.* (1928)

Ennui over the proliferation of insanity tests has spawned the proposal to abolish the insanity defense completely.[1] Some scholars have gone considerably further and urge the abolition of the defense not merely for its own sake, but as a first step toward abolishing all vestiges of *mens rea* from criminal law. Before the merits of either proposal can be considered, it is important to evaluate the two competing theories on the relationship between *mens rea* and insanity.

Mens rea, or "criminal intent," technically refers to the actor's mental state which, together with his physical act, constitutes a crime. These mental elements, as defined by the Model Penal Code and by most modern criminal codes, basically appear in four forms: (1) "Intentionally," acting toward a conscious criminal goal; (2) "Knowingly," acting with the awareness of the circumstances surrounding the act; (3) "Recklessly," acting with a conscious disregard of dangerous results known to be likely to occur; and (4) "Negligently," acting without awareness of the risk. This latter category only occurs occasionally. Any one of these four mental states constitutes *mens rea*.

Absence of any of these four mental states means that no crime has been committed, in effect, that a bodily movement occurred independently of the mind's acquiescence. The absence of *mens rea* thus establishes a claim of innocence; that is, despite the occurence of the forbidden act, there is no crime at all.

The question next arises, however, as to whether insanity negates *mens rea;* that is, whether *mens rea* implies both free- dom of will and sanity so that proof of insanity would *ipso facto* disprove a culpable *mens rea.* An affirmative position on this issue would effectively mean that insanity and *mens rea* are incompatible legal concepts which cannot coexist because they are contradictory.

The notion that insanity and *mens rea* cannot coexist is rooted in the belief that *mens rea* always necessarily embraces an element of moral culpability. The historical term *mens rea* certain- ly carries moral connotations, especially in its frequent English translation, "guilty mind." Indeed, moral blameworthiness is the idea behind the legal maxim, "Actus non facit reum, nisi mens sit rea," or, in Blackstone's translation "(A)n unwarrantable act with- out a vicious will is no crime at all."[2] The requirement of the "guilty mind" or the "vicious will" historically has been the device by which the criminal law focuses solely on the blameworthy rather than on innocent wrongdoers.[3] The insanity tests may thus be thought of as defining a group of individuals so different from their fellows as not to merit criminal sanctions.[4] That this difference consists primarily of an incapacity to appreciate immoral conduct appears in the fact that legal insanity is most often defined as the inability to distinguish right from wrong. If those who possess *mens rea* are blameworthy and those who are insane are not, then the conclusion that *mens rea* and insanity cannot coexist becomes inescapable.

Indeed, there are major cases that once seemed to support that conclusion. In *Davis* v. *United States,*[5] a reasonable doubt of the defendant's sanity is taken as a reasonable doubt of the defend- ant's guilt. Sanity is seen as essential as the overt *actus reus:* "Sanity is guilt; insanity is innocence." In this view the killing of another person cannot be committed with malice or even with intent unless the defendant comprehends the criminality of such an act. Much earlier, even Blackstone, who placed the burden of proof on the insane defendant, saw a "sound mind and discre- tion" as essential to murder; a free act and a free will are prerequisites "to a complete crime recognizable by human laws."[6] As the *Davis* court concluded, in words later embodied in *In re Winship*:

> Insanity is not in confession and avoidance, for it is a plea that controverts the existence of every fact essential to constitute the crime charged. Upon that plea the accused may stand, shielded by the presumption of his innocence, until it appears that he is guilty; and his guilt cannot in the very nature of things be regarded as proved, if the jury entertains a reasonable doubt from all the evidence of whether he was legally capable of committing the crime.[7]

One of the most explicit recent statements of the coalescence theory of *mens rea* and insanity is *United States v. Currens*.[8] In that case the Court of Appeals for the Third Circuit created a test of insanity by equating that condition of mind with an incapacity to entertain *mens rea*. The court sought a way to relate mental disease to the concept of "guilty mind" in a manner that would be meaningful to a jury. To the *Currens* court, *mens rea* is rooted in the assumption that a person has the capacity to control his behavior and to choose between alternative courses of action. Anyone who lacks the capacity to choose or to control his behavior, could not, in the court's view, possess the "guilty mind" necessary for crime. The *Currens* test thus equates insanity with a lack of *mens rea;* that is, no sanity, no guilt.

Despite this considerable support, *mens rea* can just as readily be viewed as morally neutral. *Mens rea* need not refer to a morally guilty mind but only to a specific mental state contained in the definition of crimes; for example, the intent to kill is part of the *mens rea* for murder; the intent to inflict serious bodily harm is the *mens rea* for aggravated assault.

When *mens rea* in this narrow psychological sense is considered, it becomes clear that a legally insane individual can still act so as to satisfy the *mens rea* element. For example, in ordinary circumstances, assault is morally reprehensible. However, assaultive intent is not universally reprehensible, as is indicated by such defenses or justifications as duress, defense of property, or defense of self. To assert that *mens rea* always includes such an element of moral culpability involves going beyond intent, knowledge, or recklessness and invites a search for criminal motives. While some may see the goal of the criminal law as to punish only immoral conduct, it accomplishes this objective if at all not by requiring *mens rea* in the sense of a morally guilty motive, but by referring to considerations known as excuses, defenses, or justifications, and finding, further, that no such exoneration can exempt the conduct from condemnation.

This more restricted view of *mens rea* thus suggests that the precisely defined mental states developed in the Moral Penal Code stand independently of the broad concepts of sanity and freedom of the will. The very narrowness of these *mens rea* definitions also suggests that result, as do the many newly revised state criminal codes that have adopted a *Brawner*-like bifurcated approach to *mens rea* and insanity.

In these "policy presumption" jurisdictions such as Maine,[9] guilt is divorced from the issue of insanity. Sanity is not an element of the crime; it is relevant only when the accused seeks to avoid punishment for conduct already criminal. Insanity thus is a plea of confession and avoidance; it does not deny but rather "confesses" the crime and seeks to avoid it by excuse. Insanity thus can coexist with a criminal state of mind.

The policy presumption jurisdictions view the presumption of sanity, like the presumption of innocence, as a premise rather than a conclusion of criminal law. The presumption of sanity is as indispensable as the presumption of innocence. It is the natural and normal human condition; thus the presumption of sanity has independent weight as the common state of affairs.

The essence of the policy presumption theory appears in a scholarly statement of the last century:

> When an accused relies upon any substantive, distinct, separate, and independent matter as a defense, which is outside of, and does not necessarily constitute part of, the act or transaction with which he is charged, such as the defense of insanity...then it devolves upon him to establish such special and foreign matter by a preponderance of evidence.[10]

Under this presumption, proof of insanity does not bear upon the moral guilt or innocence of the accused. Insanity is relevant only to the avoidance of the criminal sanction. Simply put, sanity is not a fact necessary to constitute the crime charged. Instead, it is an excuse to an admitted criminal act.

Some recent Supreme Court language does support this view. In his concurring opinion in *Mullaney* v. *Wilbur*,[11] Justice Rehnquist asserted that if *mens rea* and insanity could not coexist, then *Winship* would mandate that the state prove sanity beyond a reasonable doubt. In discussing the Supreme Court's holding in *Leslie* v. *Oregon*[12] whereby the state could require the defendant to prove insanity beyond a reasonable doubt, Rehnquist stated:

> (T)he existence or nonexistence of legal insanity bears no necessary relationship to the existence or nonexistence of the required mental elements of crime. For this reason, Oregon's placement of the burden of proof on insanity on Leland...did not effect an unconstitutional shift in the state's traditional burden of proof beyond a reasonable doubt of all necessary elements of the offense.[13]

Some commentators who agree with this analysis feel that insanity does bear on *mens rea* in rare cases of "abnormal ideation," where the defendant commits a proscribed act under a radical delusion; for instance, squeezes his wife's neck thinking only of squeezing lemons. This bizarre example has led some to the conclusion that insanity does bear a necessary relationship to the existence of *mens rea* in this isolated kind of conduct. But two things appear immediately. First, this kind of bizarre example has little relevance to the real world of criminal conduct, or even to the world of mental illness. Secondly, cases of abnormal ideation or delusion disprove *mens rea* directly on its own terms, not via reference to insanity, because the intent and knowledge requirements of *mens rea* are not satisfied when the actor does *not* intend a result (as killing his wife by intending to squeeze a lemon) or does not *know* the circumstances of his conduct (that is, knowing only that he is squeezing lemons, not knowing that the lemon is his wife). These factors directly disprove the existence of *mens rea* and result in an innocence claim for that reason alone, not because of any reference to insanity. Stated differently, a person who is insane because of a cognitive delusion is acquitted not because he lacks sanity but because he lacks the statutorily required mental state.

If this be the case, criminal *mens rea* in this technical, morally-neutral sense can indeed coexist with insanity. A truly insane person can legally plan and know the consequences and circumstances of criminal conduct. Such a person thus appears to possess two separate defenses, one based on a lack of *mens rea*, the other based on a lack of sanity. In this view the insanity defense acts as a second wind or second string in the bow of a guilty defendant. As the *Brawner* court hesitantly perceived, insanity in this view is not necessarily a negation of criminal intent or knowledge or recklessness but exists apart from the defining mental state. Like the similar legal excuses of infancy and necessity, the insanity defense tacitly admits both the criminal act and the criminal *mens rea* but proceeds to invoke an exception from responsibility.[14] As Professor Fingarette has pointed out:

> The mentally disabled offender, in the typical case, *does know* the nature of his act, knows it is considered a crime, and *has* the capacity to conform his behavior to law. The trouble is that he wishes to act in a way that does not conform. This lack of intent to conform arises, at least to some material extent, out of his irrationality with respect to the relevant law, and *that* is the ground of his lessened or absent responsibility.[15]

The foregoing analysis supports two conclusions: The first is that, conceptually, the legal fates of *mens rea* and insanity are separate. Altering the insanity defense does not entail the abolition of *mens rea* or of the law's free will or sanity postulates. Hence the disutility of the widespread bellowing, exemplified in the *Brawner* case, that the insanity defense is necessary in order to retain the entire concept of free will that is at the heart of the criminal justice system.

The second conclusion is more factual: As any criminal lawyer knows, the vast majority if not all insane criminals can and do in fact actually intend or know or recklessly risk their criminal acts. To take one example which stands for many, M'Naghten himself quite obviously intended the death of the prime minister and knew that it was frowned upon by his peers. It is simply not the case that the truly insane are incapable of deliberation and moral understanding. Rather, like "wild beasts" and children, their mental operations occur within an unusually restricted arena of some misinterpreted facts, the context of which prevents the usual inhibitions from arresting the criminal plan. One might say, of course, that the insane defendant didn't "fully" or "really" know what he was doing; but such an interpretation does not cloud the fact that most insane persons exhibit knowledge and intention in the planning and executioin of the criminal act, often to the point of being overbearing.[16] In a word, insanity does not preclude a criminal *mens rea* but only suggests that it be excused, just as the age of a very young child excuses his freely chosen and conscious crimes.

If the insane are in fact conscious of their criminal behavior, such evidence properly touches on a finding of *mens rea*, not of insanity. Hence, the fate of insane persons on the guilt-innocence issue is primarily dependent upon the fate of *mens rea*, not on the role of insanity.

Chapter 9
<u>Mens Rea</u> Cannot Be Abolished

> By deleting references to purpose and intent, we might eventually come to define all crimes in terms of acts alone: as behavior, not motive.
>
> **Professor W. Gaylin**

Originally early English common law located criminal liability solely in two objective facts, namely, that an evil deed had been done and that it was the accused person who had done it. While this notion did rear its head during the early common law, the ecclesiastical influences coming to a head with Bracton caused strict liability to become almost totally abandoned in the criminal law. The ensuing maxim "actus non facit reum nisi mens sit rea" stressed the importance of moral blameworthiness as a prerequisite for liability. In the traditional view of Professor Turner, "Wickedness exists in men's minds and moral blame can only be laid upon one whose thoughts or intentions have been bad."

As a result of the positivist trend in legal thought during the nineteenth century, the ideas of responsibility and blame lost favor and *mens rea* came to be more formalistically understood as a mere psychological appendage to crime. Yet the original idea behind the Latin phrase was to exclude from liability, for example, those persons killing by misadventure or in self-defense—in other words, to restrict liability to cases where there was more than a mere intentional act causing harm forbidden by law. In the traditional view, there must be, in addition, some moral reason to reproach or blame the wrongdoer for that act.

Like their positivist ancestors, the criminological theorists from the school of legal realism who wrote in the early part of this century again revived the proposal to eliminate from the criminal law this entire *mens rea* requirement. In this version the abolition was not to be limited to these moral connotations surrounding *mens rea* but was to include the very *mens rea* concept itself. Every form of motive or intention was to be eliminated, so that the issue of guilt would reduce itself simply to the question of whether the offending act alone had occurred. While complex, the overriding motivation of this school of thought appears in retrospect to be one of social defense. The security of the group was placed above that of the individual: Antisocial conduct must be punished apart from whatever intention, good or bad, coexisted with it.

This position continues to echo today, and some of its proponents are illustrious.

Lady Barbara Wootton has argued that *mens rea* must be abolished because there is really no way to undertstand a person's mind and see intent at work.[1] Karl Menninger has argued that all crime is really a sickness, and there is no point in discussing a sick mind in a criminal trial.[2] Professor W. Gaylin takes a similar view:

> The solution, I think, might be to move precisely opposite to the current trend. Instead of introducing more psychological concepts into the law, we should remove as many as possible. Indeed in many instances this is already done; most of civil law and many minor crimes are defined without reference to intent. One can be guilty of a parking violation irrespective of one's good intentions about putting an extra dime in the meter. By deleting references to purpose and intent, we might eventually come to define all crimes in terms of acts alone: as behavior, not motive. An impossible goal? Perhaps, but impossible goals often indicate rewarding directions.[3]

Wootton's thesis is perhaps the most instructive and should be considered in some detail. Lady Wootton draws on her experience as a magistrate and social scientist to argue that the insanity defense itself should be abolished because psychiatrists are incapable of determining whether the accused, at the time of the crime, could not, or merely would not, conform his conduct to the law. Wootton premises her argument on the theory that our current system of criminal law based on punishment of the wicked is outdated. There is no distinction, she argues, between a crime that is *malum in se* and one which is *malum prohibitum*, a classic conclusion for legal positivism. Furthermore, the promulgation of new strict liability offenses makes the distinction useless. She concludes:

> [T]he presence or absence of the guilty mind is [not] unimportant, but...*mens rea* has, so to speak—and this is the crux of the matter—*got* [sic] *into the wrong place*. Traditionally, the requirement of the guilty mind is written into the actual definition of a crime. No guilty intention, no crime, is the rule. Obviously this makes sense if the law's concern is with wickedness: Where there is no guilty intention, there can be no wickedness. But it is equally obvious, on the other hand, that an action does not become innocuous merely because whoever performed it meant no harm. If the object of the criminal law is to prevent the occurrence of socially damaging actions, it would be absurd to turn a blind eye to those which were due to carelessness, negligence, or even accident. The question of motivation is *in the first instance* irrelevant.

Wootton thus argues that, instead of punishing the "evil-minded," the criminal justice system should prevent future criminal behavior by isolating and, if possible, predicting those persons inclined toward socially unacceptable behavior. If the primary purpose of the system is to prevent crime, it is illogical, she argues, to confine this preventioin to occasions where forbidden acts are done with special states of mind. Mental state is irrelevant; it is the criminal act and its punishment and prevention that become all important. The commission of an offending act would trigger the maneuvering of a "treatment tribunal" empowered to weigh a number of individual and social factors, including the likelihood of future dangerous behavior and the likely effect of a particular sentence in reforming the offender.

Wootton's thesis is perhaps the clearest statement of the abolitionist proposal. Under her approach defendants would not be "blamed" but rather "treated" for committing antisocial acts. The varieties of treatment could run the gamut from immediate unconditional release to a lifetime commitment in either a prison or a hospital, with a wide range of dispositions in between.[4]

Proposals such as Wootton's are not directed precisely at insanity; they seek to eliminate all evidence of mental state from the criminal law so as to replace the subjective concepts of guilt, blame, free will, and responsibility with the simpler, more objective concept of social danger.

The late Herbert Packer has suggested several of the likely assumptions that underlie this social defense system of criminal law:

1. Free will is an illusion because human conduct is determined by forces that lie beyond the individual's power to modify.

2. Moral responsibility,. accordingly, is an illusion because blame cannot be ascribed for behavior that is ineluctably conditioned.

3. Human conduct, being causally determined, can, and should be, scientifically studied and controlled.

4. The function of the criminal law should be purely and simply to bring into play processes for modifying the personality and hence the behavior of people who commit antisocial acts, so that they will not commit them in the future; or, if all else fails, to restrain them from committing offenses by the use of external compulsion (for instance, confinement).

5. We have...real knowledge about how to rehabilitate people.

6. We know how to predict those who exhibit traits that are dangerous.[5]

The advocates of this streamlined, behavioral criminal law see it as more scientific, manageable, and forward-looking than the traditional punishment-oriented, free will system rooted in the classical concept of *mens rea*.

From a careful analysis, however, there appear a number of cogent reasons why *mens rea* cannot be abolished, even in its modern limited psychological sense. At the phenomenological level, *mens rea* in its traditional sense of "blame" is simply a legalistic way of enshrining certain interpretative concepts that operate effectively in everyday noncriminal contexts. *Mens rea* crystallizes the pervasive but elusive rationale of responsibility based on an assessment of purpose. In the everyday world, people have goals, direct means to ends, and anticipate the consequences of their acts. When a person is shoved in a crowd, for example, the "shovee's" response to the "shover" depends entirely upon whether the shove is interpreted as deliberate or accidental.

Similarly, punishment and administrative consequences differ for a person who causes an automobile accident through either recklessness or through some uncontrollable mechanical defect. Within the criminal law, the *mens rea* concept adopts these everyday assumptions for interpreting equivocal behavior. *Mens rea* thus is rooted not so much in legal history as in human history, in the everyday working predication of merit and blame based on interpretation of intentionality. A public trial thus may seem analogous to a public morality play serving to underscore the everyday concept of intentionality as a valid criterion for evaluating behavior. *Mens rea* becomes a reminder that human society is a commune, not merely a collection of physical bodies moving as vectors. We interpret and discover the intentionality of other people in and through their words and deeds, and judge them primarily on the basis of their intentions. Abolition of *mens rea* from the law would not abolish it from the everyday world of human interaction.[6]

To this phenomenological analysis must be added a further, more legalistic reason for retaining the present concept of *mens rea:* Abolition of *mens rea* creates strict liability for all conduct, with crimes reduced to ambiguous bodily acts. Manslaughter becomes inseparable from homicide. The various degrees of murder would necessarily be abolished. Tax fraud would become no different than an error in arithmetic and, of course, vice versa. Inchoate crimes like conspiracy would disappear. Many crimes would merge with torts: assault, battery, and false imprisonment would be indistinguishable as crimes or torts, with a curious difficulty in distinguishing the propriety of dollar damages from the propriety of incarceration. Most criminals would become tortfeasors and vice versa, and much of the law of crime would merge with the law of torts, for the habitually negligent hardly offer more solace to society than do the occasionally criminal. Wootton herself consistently admits that no distinction can be made between the "mad" and the "bad" or between penal and medical institutions.

Wootton's strict liability thus coalesces exactly with B.F. Skinner's notion that it is not the person's attitude but the environment which needs both the blame and the change.[7]

To this Clockwork Orange scenario is a further objection. The public experiences the much-debated "free will myth" in certain central acts like long-range planning and resistance to negative conditioning. Human beings repeatedly experience their freedom to choose. This experience, valid or not from a laboratory pigeon's perspective, supports postulating free will at the vestibule of the criminal law. Even if scientific analysis sees free will as an illusion, it is an illusion that all persons experience and which the criminal law necessarily reinforces if it is to be consistent with that experience.[8]

The proposal to abolish *mens rea* becomes impractical for yet another reason. It substitutes for "bad" and "mad" the nebulous concept of "social deviancy." It would subject to government control not only the bad and the mad but all tortfeasors, idealist reformers, and eccentrics—in a word, all nonconformists. This kind of law encroaches on all, for once guilt is abolished, so too is innocence. The difficulty with a criminal policy based on social deviancy is its underlying assumption of an infallible, static society which must march in step forevermore. Such people as Martin Luther King, Daniel Berrigan, and Henry David Thoreau differ in degree and in kind from the violent armed robber and rapist. With the abolition of *mens rea,* criminal law would lose its discriminating index of culpability and confuse social nonconformity with criminality. Despite Wootton's deterministic assumption that crime is a unilateral bodily concept, the fact is that a wide chasm separates a genetic compulsion to crime such as the XYY chromosome from deliberate, prolonged defiance to a detested law as in the instance of war protestors or civil rights activists. Neither of these scenarios covers the more commonplace situation where crime reflects a spontaneous attempt to capitalize on an immediate opportunity, as in most burglaries and auto thefts. The point is that for each type of crime mental states vary and this variation dictates varying degrees of culpability. If mental states become either a unilateral or a nonexistent concept in defining criminality, the severity of the crime, the defendant's culpability, and the propreity of treatment cannot be determined.

Finally, there is the question of the constitutionality of the Wootton proposal. Lady Wootton has stressed that the concept of "strict liability" already exists in Anglo-Saxon criminal law and could reasonably be expanded. She makes much of the fact that in England there is at least one serious crime, the offense of "causing death by dangerous driving," that has no element of intent. Based on this one instance, she sees no reason why other crimes need intent. But in this country the United States Supreme Court has been zealous in maintaining the concept of *mens rea* as the general rule. As the District of Columbia Court of Appeals said in *United States* v. *Brawner,*

> [W]hile, as noted in *Morrisette,* the legislature has dispensed with the mental element in some statutory offenses, in furtherance of a paramount need of the community, these instances mark the exception and not the rule, and only in the most limited instances has the mental element been omitted by the legislature as a requisite for an offense that was a crime at common law.[9]

It is unlikely that the abolition of *mens rea* could square with the constitutional requirements of due process and equal protection.

For all these reasons, the suggestion to abolish *mens rea* from the criminal law is impractical.

Chapter 10

Insanity as a Statutory Element and as an Excuse

> Cognition is not the complement of volition; it is its precursor.
>
> H. Packer

Ordinarily, in the criminal law sanity is presumed. A defendant's motivation is usually irrelevant to this assumption; for instance, the fact that a defendant genuinely believed that a fatal act was morally justified in order to end oppression is ordinarily irrelevant to guilt or innocence.

Such a scenario, however, does not fit the circumstance of insanity. Here motivation is clearly relevant to a determination of sanity's absence. Motivation is a window on the defendant's state of mind. But is it the motivation or the insane state itself which excuses? Or, put differently, is sanity a condition of culpability and insanity an excuse?

There is an obvious conceptual difference between treating the insane as a large class universally exempt by definition from culpability like infants, and treating an insane person as a solitary individual excused only for a particular act. The first instance trades on the analogy between insanity and infancy and suggests that insanity is an objective exemption for an entire human category apart from any inquiry into motivation. The second instance trades on the notion that insanity is like duress and deserves a special exemption, if at all, only for the bizarre motivation of one individual at a time. If insanity is a general exemption like infancy, it should be raised at the outset of a criminal case as a threshold challenge to the jurisdiction of the court to hear the case. If, on the other hand, it is an excuse, then insanity bears on liability only after other evidence first establishes that an accused individual did in fact perform some prohibited act.

To assist in approaching these conceptual issues it may be helpful to divide exoneration in the criminal law into three general categories of defenses: (1) element of the crime defenses; (2) justifications; and (3) excuses.[1]

Element of the crime defenses or, as Robinson and others[2] describe them, "failure of proof defenses," consist of instances in which the required statutory elements of an offense cannot be proven in court. The reason for the failure of proof is usually either insufficient or contradictory evidence. Whatever the reason, a defense based on a failure to prove an element of the crime results in an acquittal because the prosecution's evidence falls short of the required statutory definition of the crime.

Justification defenses are different; they are not evidentiary shortcomings in proof. They operate to exempt certain criminal conduct from culpability because the criminal harm is considered outweighed by a greater social good. Justification defenses involve circumstances preexisting the criminal conduct: a fire which must be put out, or unruly students who must be disciplined. Legally justified conduct appears as a necessary response to the preexisting threat. It must also be portioned to it; for instance, a teacher may spank but not maim unruly students. In cases where these requirements are met, the defense of justification condones rather than condemns the criminal conduct. Robinson illustrates the point as follows:

> A forest fire rages toward a town of 10,000 unsuspecting inhabitants. The actor burns a field of corn located between the fire and the town; the burned field then serves as a firebreak, saving 10,000 lives. The actor has satisfied all elements of the offense of arson by setting fire to the field with the purpose of destroying it. The immediate harm he has caused—the destruction of the field—is precisely the harm which the statute serves to prevent and punish. Yet the actor is likely to have a complete defense because his conduct and its harmful consequences were justified. The conduct in this instance is tolerated, even encouraged, by society.[3]

The third category of exoneration, that of excuse, is unlike defenses based on elements of the crime and on justification. Whereas justified conduct is legitimate behavior which is generally tolerated, an excuse suggests that, though the conduct is wrong, liability is inappropriate because of some unique characteristic of the particular actor. Whereas justificaiton defenses view the act, defenses based on excuse view the individual actor. A justification defense eliminates guilt *ab initio;* an excuse defense admits wrongful conduct but seeks an individual exemption in the actor's personal makeup. Excuses admit that the deed is wrong but exempt the actor because of a personal disability not widely shared in the community. The disability is usually an objective condition with observable traits. It may be long or short term, permanent or temporary, physical or mental. In each case, however, the excuse resides in some individual defect in cognition, as in the case of mistake, or in volition, as in the case of duress.

These three modes of exoneration based on the failure to prove an element of the crime, justification, and excuse reflect differing social interests. Elements of the crime defenses are not defenses over and above the statutory definition of a crime. Recognition of this defense in court does not therefore undermine the broad deterrent purpose of the criminal law. Conduct which is justified also exhibits no social evil to condemn. Though a harm may have been committed, justification acquittals announce that the act in question achieved, or sought to achieve, a social good greater than the evil prohibited by the criminal statute.

Excuses, however, present a strikingly narrower public policy rationale. Excuses do tend to undermine the general and special deterrent purposes of the penal law. The rationale for acquittal based on excuse is also much less apparent than it is in justification or in the failure of element defenses. Often only a juror or trial spectator can appreciate the fact that the excuse is based on the unique characteristics of the actor, not on a blanket approval of the act.

In this threefold classification, then, what sort of defense is insanity? It clearly is not a justification defense. It clearly is an excuse. In addition, when its presence negates the required mental element of a crime, insanity also constitutes a defense based on a failure to prove an element of the crime. In either aspect, it is not a general, *a priori* jurisdictional exemption like infancy, but a special exception like duress.

As a failure of proof defense, the insanity defense is sometimes called partial responsibility or diminished capacity. These terms emphasize the notion that this defense falls short of insanity. When there are lesser degrees of culpability, as in the case of homicide, mental illness may reduce the defendant's liability to a lesser degree of the original offense. However, there is nothing partial about the defense itself. Mental defect either negates the required statutory element or it does not. In the process it either does or does not succeed in providing a defense to the original offense charged.[4]

As an excuse defense, insanity exempts an individual from an acknowledged criminal act. This exemption resides in the humane conviction that it is fundamentally unfair to penalize a person for conduct stemming uncontrollably from a volitional or cognitive defect. But beyond this, insanity exists as an excuse different in kind from all other excuses recognized in the criminal law. When the excuse of mistake is involved, for example, exoneration resides in the notion that the mistaken defendant nonetheless acted reasonably and if he continues to do so in the future, the social consequences are not likely to be detrimental because of the implicit good faith that has been shown. Where the excuse of insanity is involved, however, there is no such ready assurance that socially harmful conduct will never recur. Furthermore, other excuses also involve objectively verifiable conditions, such as physical impairment or measurable intoxication or the presence of coercion. In the case of insanity, objective verification is less compelling—indeed, strikingly different conclusions may be drawn from the same medical facts.

The law of excuses acknowledges that human frailty produces results beyond human control. The case for some form of insanity defense rests on the protection of human autonomy, not on crime prevention. The excuse of insanity recognizes that responsibility is the appropriate criterion for limiting the reach of criminal intervention. Put another way, the rationale for excuses generally, and insanity in particular, is that the law should punish only in cases of controllable misdeeds. When the actor's freedom of choice is constricted by insanity, no truly human act occurs because there is no truly human volition involved.

However, the legal rationale for some form of insanity defense does not resolve the social concern over its application. The public increasingly questions the viability of the excuse function of the insanity defense in light of the deterrent purposes of the criminal law. One of the major functions of the criminal law is to act as a safety valve on community sentiment by giving the public an occasion to vent its horror and disapproval. The important social interests in condemnation and deterrence which are thought to be protected by the special verdict of insanity are necessarily endangered in any excuse based on subjectively excusing conditions not readily understandable by the public at large. A socially sound approach would minimize public misperception of the excuse by helping the public grasp the unique and limited nature of the exception from liability. The solution is not a total aboliton of the defense but some mode of reformulation of its excuse message.

Chapter 11

Which Formulation
of the Insanity Test Is Best?

"For every Ph.D. there is an equal and opposite Ph.D."

—Anon.

At least four recent efforts have surfaced to redefine the test for insanity; each deserves mention.

1. Insanity as an affirmative defense

Some observers, desiring to separate authentic from sham insanity claims, urge that whatever its linguistic formulation, the defense should be defined procedurally as an affirmative burden which the defendant must carry.[1] One legislative motivation for making the defendant prove his own insanity appears to be to make the defense less effective; another motive is to simplify courtroom procedures.

Under present law, if the defendant raises the issue of insanity the government bears the burden of proving beyond a reasonable doubt that the defendant was not insane at the time the crime was committed. This burden was first placed on the prosecution by the Supreme Court in 1895, in a departure from the common law rule under which the burden of proof for all affirmative defenses, including insanity, rested with the defendant.

Placing the burden of proof on the defendant is constitutionally permissible, so long as it does not relieve the prosecution from its obligation of proving the required mental state. This approach, however, would perpetuate the insanity defense in its present form and would continue to permit the acquittal of persons whose acts are prohibited by the criminal law. It would still permit the introduction of confusing psychiatric testimony. Jury instructions regarding the location and weight of burdens of proof would be further complicated. In short, this sort of tinkering would make no impact on the major issues. That fact coupled with the increased procedural complexity suggests that such a change is little more than window dressing, as Attorney General William Smith himself has admitted.

2. The bifurcated trial

A second suggested legislative reform involves the use of a bifurcated trial in which the issues of guilt and sanity are tried separately, with the trial on guilt coming first, to be followed by a second trial on insanity. The new Maine criminal code allows such a procedure at the option of the defendant.[2] In whatever formulation, the bifurcated trial concept implies that guilt can be fully determined without an inquiry into the sanity of the accused. Bifurcation also raises the hope that relegating psychiatric evidence to the insanity phase of the trial would leave the jury's consideration of guilt less encumbered by expert medical testimony.

The central thesis in this bifurcation proposal rests on the asserted evidenciary separability of guilt and mental state; that is, on the assumption that evidence of sanity can be segregated from evidence bearing on intention, knowledge, and recklessness. That is a dubious hope at best. In recent years, several jurisdictions have ruled that such a bifurcated procedure fails to comply with due process guarantees. The highest courts of Arizona, Wyoming, and Florida[3] have declared their bifurcation statutes unconstitutional. With greater than usual unanimity these courts have reasoned that if evidence of the accused's insanity is considered only after guilt, a conclusive presumption of sanity arises in the first trial. This presumption operates to deny the accused the opportunity to have all the facts needed for guilt presented prior to a finding of guilt. Thus a defendant is under a "suspended" but "presumed" status of guilt until the jury considers the insanity defense.[4]

California sought to resolve this aspect of the due process problem by distinguishing between evidence of mental illness which negated *mens rea* and similar evidence that established insanity. The former would be admitted in the first phase of the trial, while evidence showing incapacity to form *mens rea* would be introduced only in the second phase.[5] While this format seeks to comply with the due process requirements regarding the presumption of innocence and *mens rea*, the entire justification for bifurcation is undermined, for there is no workable bar to introducing psychiatric evidence indicating a lack of *mens rea* while defending on the merits in the first trial. The California distinction, in a word, is unworkable.

A resulting problem involves the economics of time. A bifurcated procedure essentially involves duplicate trials. The second trial becomes repetitive of the first because psychiatric evidence indicating a lack of *mens rea* is essentially the same as the evidence proving that the defendant was insane at the time of the offense. Due process demands the admission of psychiatric evidence relevant to the determination of guilt. Bifurcated trials serve to force admission of this evidence in two trials rather than one. In the end, a bifurcated procedure will not work because it is repetitive, and to the extent that it ceases to be repetitive, it is unconstitutional.

3. "Guilty but mentally ill"

A recently suggested approach to modifying the insanity defense calls for a special verdict of "guilty but mentally ill" (GBMI). The attorney general's Task Force on Violent Crime recommended this approach in its final report, and several midwestern states have enacted legislation to this effect. This reform leaves the existing defense of insanity intact but permits the GBMI verdict as an alternative where a defendant pleading insanity suffers from a mental illness not so serious as to qualify for legal insanity. It is intended to be an addition to the insanity scenario rather than a replacement—at least in principle.

Michigan offers the most researched example of this verdict. In that state, a criminal defendant may be found guilty, nonguilty, not guilty by reason of insanity, or, finally, GBMI. The GBMI verdict is intended to identify defendants who are mentally ill but not legally insane. Such a defendant is subjected to a psychiatric examination before being imprisoned. The effect of the scheme, ideally, is to mandate increased attention to the psychiatric needs of those found GBMI.

Following Michigan's lead, Indiana and Illinois have amended their criminal procedure laws in order to permit a finding of GBMI whenever a defendant pleads the insanity defense. Their provisions are similar to Michigan's: a defendant found GBMI is sentenced as if he were convicted of the crime charged but is offered psychiatric examination and treatment, if available, before completion of his penal sentence.[6]

In whatever formulation, to GBMI verdict in each state thus operates as a supplement to the insanity defense. It carves out a portion of those who might successfully invoke that defense. Indeed, for those found GBMI, the only effective difference from a guilty verdict lies in the requirement of medical attention during incarceration. The new verdict offers an alternative to the stark choice of innocence and guilt and thus presents the jury with a point of compromise; by a means of providing a recognition of penal responsibility while assuring some consideration of the defendant's mental state at the sentencing stage. In short, it raises an appealing compromise verdict to an indecisive jury.

Observations of experimental juries have revealed that the GBMI verdict appears as a convenient compromise many jurors prefer. Such a compromise could occur either where jurors who favor conviction on a greater offense split their differences with jurors who favor acquittal, or where the jury simply takes the easier course of compromise rather than fully debating the defendant's claim of insanity. Especially in serious cases, jurors hesitate to accept the insanity defense for fear that an acquittal would result in the defendant's immediate reappearance on the streets. Conversely, a finding of unqualified guilt may also be unappealing because of sympathy for a defendant's mental problems.

Problems abound. In the first place, GBMI offers no clear distinction between mental illness and insanity. Although defendants in Michigan have argued that the definitions of mental illness and insanity are so vague as to confer unlimited discretion, the real problem is that juries are not given sufficient criteria to distinguish between the degree of illness justifying GBMI as opposed to not guilty because of insanity. Secondly, the GBMI statutes are bottomed on the notion of a compromise verdict. If, however, the insanity defense is an important moral ingredient in the law, then the reasons against its direct abolition also argue against an indirect, de facto abolition through the GBMI verdict. Third, the GBMI verdict procedures intend to insure that a mentally ill offender receive treatment. There are, however, far more effective ways of insuring treatment than by turning that medical decision over to a lay jury. Finally, as Michigan's experience has shown, the GBMI verdict is no assurance whatsoever of actual psychiatric attention in prison.

In the long run, the contention that the GBMI verdict eliminates the practical availability of the traditional insanity verdict is the most serious. If public sentiment against the insanity defense represents the mood of the majority of jurors, it is quite likely that insanity acquittals will decline in number as GBMI verdicts increase, as has occurred in Michigan—a legislative triumph, of sorts, but one achieved through the nearly total practical abolition of the traditional insanity defense. Though efforts can be made to prevent jury abuse, and subtle distinctions between mental illness and insanity may perhaps be made, the combination of the existing suspicion toward insanity and the difficulty of determining its degrees makes it difficult to see how truly insane defendants can avoid being sent to prison under the GBMI rubric. If other states' experiences duplicate Michigan's in showing a decline in insanity verdicts proportionate to the number of GBMI verdicts, there will exist grounds for a constitutional claim that the latter has eviscerated, if not negated, the former.

4. Abolition of the defense

According to former President Richard Nixon, the insanity defense provides a ready escape for ingenious criminals. His views originate apparently in the story of a defendant accused of aircraft piracy who boasted that he could manipulate his trial by feigning mental illness.[7] Nixon wished to curb such "unconscionable abuses" by proposing a federal criminal statute providing that mental diseases or defects would not constitute a defense unless the defendant lacked the state of mind required as an element of the offense charged.[8] Nixon termed this proposal "the most significant feature" of the new code. Persons found not guilty by reason of insanity would be detained for long periods in mental hospitals, about which apparently Nixon was not concerned. Instead, he focused on patients who were expeditiously released by psychiatric staff members who determined that their hospitalization had resulted from fabricated defenses and from overly credulous juries.

In addition to Mr. Nixon's unique rationale, at least three other contemporary motivations urge the complete abolition of the defense.

In the first place, the seemingly unreasonable acquittals of defendants such as Hinckley suggest that the insanity defense is a sham and/or legal technicality exploitable at the expense of public security.[9] Secondly, more sophisticated courtroom observers witness the spectacle of judicial proceedings being debased by overbearing psychiatric testimony, usually on both sides, which suggests that the *legal* determination of responsibility is, at bottom, only an arbitrary *medical* assessment.[10] These observers argue that abolition of psychologists and psychiatrists from the courtroom could best be accomplished by abolishing the insanity defense in its entirety. Thirdly, some legally oriented commentators have observed that all the varying tests are at best redundant and are at worst too confusing and archaic for the modern jury to apply. Again, an abolition of the defense appears to this group as the best way to abolish these language problems.[11]

Whatever may be the partial merits of these motivations for abolishing the insanity defense, a complete abolition poses formidable problems. Apart for its varying linguistic formulations, the insanity defense in some form is required by both legal precedent and humane considérations. Outright abolition would not likely square either with the courts or with our consciences.

From the standpoint of conscience alone, human experience always excuses conduct which is uncontrollable. We assess both reward and blame on the common ground of individual merit. We speak of both good and evil persons receiving what they "deserve," thereby implying that it is their own chosen conduct which determines their desserts.[12] At bottom, as P. Ricoeur[13] and others have shown phenomenologically, human experience suggests that reward and punishment are visited only on persons who so control their conduct that they could have done otherwise—or, as Dostoevski put it, "Notre demon est la measure de notre ange;" that is, one deserves credit for doing good only because that person could just as well have not done so. Neither reward nor punishment is appropriate for a person truly deprived of the power to control his conduct.

These considerations reside in our human nature above and beyond legal precedent. The insane defendant is simply too far removed from normality to generate justifiable anger. Rendering such a person criminally responsible makes that person suffer without any prospect of deterrence. The other theories of punishment such as retribution and rehabilitation also envision persons capable of choosing how they behave. They therefore find no application in persons unable to choose. The example of punishing the insane undermines the common notion that people should only be punished for what they can help doing.[14] These humane insights are at work not only in insanity but in other areas of "accidental" human conduct, whether caused by a heart attack, epilepsy, duress, sleepwalking, or other powers beyond human control. Each serves as a reminder that the measure of culpability is limited by the measure of cognitive control.

Established law reflects and formalizes these humanistic insights. As shown in earlier chapters, the concept that the insane should not be held responsible for criminal acts is firmly embedded in the earliest Judeo-Christian laws. Criminal liability for most offenses has always resided in moral turpitude. From the earliest common law, insanity in some form has been either a partial or complete defense. The legal defense was firmly established by the time the United States Constitution was adopted, and it has remained a fundamental part of American criminal law since Revolutionary days. The due process clause of the Fourteenth Amendment intends in part to protect fundamental rights long recognized under the common law. Because it is so basic to the American legal system, the insanity defense in some form is probably protected by that amendment. The insanity defense operates to ensure that the mentally ill offender will receive psychiatric care and treatment in a nonpunitive setting. Punishing the insane is a legal *non sequitur.* As Judge Kaufman noted in *United States* v. *Freeman,*[15] the punishment of the mentally ill is inconsistent with the moral sense of the community:

> The criminal law, it has been said, is an expression of the moral sense of the community. The fact that the law has, for centuries, regarded certain wrongdoers as improper subjects for punishment is a testament to the extent to which that moral sense has developed. Thus, society has recognized over the years that none of the three asserted purposes of the criminal law—rehabilitation, deterrence, and retribution—is satisfied when the truly irresponsible...are punished.
>
> What rehabilitative function is served when one who is mentally incompetent and found guilty is ordered to serve a sentence in prison? Is not the curative or restorative function better achieved in such a case in an institution designed and equipped to treat just such individuals? And how is deterrence achieved by punishing the incompetent? Those who are substantially unable to restrain their conduct are, by definition, undeterrable and their "punishment" is no example for others; those who are unaware of, or do not appreciate the nature and quality of, their actions can hardly be expected rationally to weigh the consequences of their

conduct. Finally, what segment of society can feel its desire for retribution satisfied when it wreaks vengeance upon the incompetent? Although an understandable emotion, a need for retribution can never be permitted in a civilized society to degenerate into a sadistic form of revenge.

In addition to the practical reasons for the insanity defense, its retention appears constitutionally required. Eliminating it has been held unconstitutional.[16] Washington and Mississippi are the only jurisdictions that have faced the constitutional issues square-ly.[17] The highest courts in both jurisdictions have held that an unqualified elimination of the defense violates state constitution-al provisions relating to due process. They reasoned that sanity is a condition precedent to the capacity to form intent; it is therefore an essential element of guilt.[18] Due process requires that when the issue of a defendant's insanity is raised the jury find the defendant sane at the time of the charged offense in order to return a guilty verdict.

In *State* v. *Strasburg*, the Washington Supreme Court also held that an elimination of that state's defense of insanity violated the defendant's state constitutional right to a jury trial. The court noted that:

> [T]his right of trial by jury which our Constitution declares shall remain inviolate must mean something more than the preservation of the mere form of trial by jury, else the legislature could by a process of elimination in defining crime or criminal procedure entirely destroy the substance of the right by limiting the questions of fact to be submitted to the jury.[19]

The elimination of the insanity defense could result in the imprisonment of a defendant who was insane when the offense was committed. Imprisonment would amount to punishing as a criminal someone not responsible and, as such, would raise a serious issue of cruel and unusual punishment under the Eighth Amendment.[20]

This reasoning was advanced in *Sinclair* v. *State* where the Mississippi Supreme Court held unconstitutional a statute elimi-nating the insanity defense for the charge of murder. The concur-ring opinion of Judge Ethridge (joined by two other judges) reasoned that:

The provisions of the state and federal constitutions prohibiting cruel and unusual punishments were designed to protect the people, not only from barbarious methods of inflicting punishment, but to prevent harsh, unjust, and unreasonable punishments, considering the act prohibited in relation to the punishment imposed. In other words, it may be perfectly permissible to inflict life imprisonment or death for murder when done with malice aforethought, yet it would be utterly unreasonable and unjust and inhuman to punish a petty misdemeanor with life imprisonment or death. It certainly would be cruel and unusual to punish a child of tender years, incapable of judging the consequences of its act, should it, through misjudgment or otherwise, administer poison to another child or to another person. It would be equally cruel and equally as unusual to impose life imprisonment or death upon any person who did not have intelligence enough to know that the act was wrong or to know the consequences that would likely result from the act.[21]

For these reasons, the insanity defense cannot be totally abolished. The ultimate solution is not the abolition of the entire defense but a reformulation of its language by purging the test of any medical ideology.

5. Keep the defense; abolish the test

Ennui over the invasion of medical experts into the courtroom, the acquittals of persons like Hinckley, and the witch and warlock atmosphere of insanity trials have prompted many frustrated academics and practitioners to support Mr. Nixon's recommendation for the complete abolition of the defense. For the humane and constitutional reasons already seen above, the defense itself cannot be totally abolished. What can be effectively abolished, however, is any and all special statutory tests for determing insanity. In its place, insanity evidence should simply be admissible to the extent, if any, that it disproves the statutory mental state defining the crime that the defendant is being charged with; that is, to the extent that it disproves intent, knowledge, recklessness, or negligence.

The abolition of a specific test language offends neither the Constitution nor case law as long as *mens rea* remains. It could enlist approval from linguists, medical specialists, and the general public. Such a device would reinsert the insanity defense into its proper historical context prior to *M'Naghten* and, at the same time, relate it properly to the narrowly defined Model Penal Code definitions of *mens rea*. From a medical standpoint, the abolition of all test language would recognize two things: first, the fact that insanity is not a rigid state but a matter of fluctuation in insight; and secondly, the fact that any legal test of insanity incorporating medical concepts is thereby limited to passing medical ideology and is therefore unable to accommodate changing theories of illness.

No statement of a rule permitting relevant evidence of mental defect or disease on the issue of *mens rea* should be required. Relevant evidence on the mental element of a crime is already clearly admissible. A clear statement of the role of insanity evidence is required, however, to insure that the traditional tests do not survive and to indicate that such evidence relates only to the special *mens rea* requirement at the time of the criminal act. Such a statement might be phrased thus:

> All evidence relevant to the issue of *mens rea,* including evidence of mental defect or disease existing at the time of the act, shall be admissible. Such evidence shall be considered with respect to either general *mens rea* or any special mental element required either for the crime charged or any included crime. Except as provided herein, mental defect or disease does not constitute a defense,[22]

or, perhaps more precisely,

> In any prosecution for an offense, evidence that the defendant suffered from a mental disease or defect may be offered by the defendant whenever it is relevant to negative: (a) the culpable mental state required for the commission of the offense charged; or (b) the minimal requirement for crimiinal liability as specified in this code,[23]

or, as the proposed federal criminal code recommends:

> It is a defense to a prosecution under any federal statute that the defendant, as a result of mental disease or defect, lacked the state of mind required as an element of the offense charged. Mental disease or defect does not otherwise constitute a defense.[24]

These kinds of statements insure the admissibility of evidence of mental defect on the issue of *mens rea*, but abolish the insanity defense as an excuse independent of *mens rea*. This is not abolition in the complete sense of the short-lived Washington,[25] Mississippi,[26] or Louisiana[27] statutes, which would have precluded all evidence of mental defect even on the issue of *mens rea*.[28] Instead, it is the abolition of the endless tests, definitions, and redefinitions that have reduced insanity trials to an arena for editorialists and a linguistic orgy for psychiatrists.

Admittedly, this proposal explicitly changes the historical duality of insanity previously discussed in chapter 10 where insanity appeared both as a *mens rea* defense and as an excuse separate from *mens rea*. In the view proposed here, the defense disappears as a "second wind" and survives only insofar as it negates the required mental element for the offense. Under this proposal, insanity constitutes a failure of proof or "absence of an element" defense, and nothing more. The excuse or "confession and avoidance" theory of insanity disappears. Perhaps more accurately, the excusing insanity evidence merges into the *mens rea* determination, so that the jury need only decide if the evidence of insanity negates the required mental state defined by the statute. As the excuse function of insanity disappears, so too would the special verdict of acquittal and thereby the implied permissiveness announced by such a verdict.

The difference may appear at first as largely conceptual, perhaps the short of hairsplitting that law review articles feed upon. The prosecutor's burden of showing insanity, *actus reus*, and *mens rea* of course remains; however, there are important changes. The use of specific insanity test language and a corresponding jury instruction would disappear. The scope of the admitted evidence narrows to the defendant's mental state only at the time of the crime. A social difference also arises from the abolition of the excuse function of insanity. The conduct in an excuse constitutes a net harm deserving prohibition. Abolition of the excuse function, and the corresponding abolition of the special verdict, would announce to the public that insanity apart from its relevance to *mens rea* does not merit exemption from the criminal sanction.

Adoption of these provisions would effectively eliminate the insanity defense as a prolonged battleground of experts. In a murder trial, for example, the focus of the inquiry would be as follows, "At the time of the act, did the defendant intend to kill the victim?" rather than "Could this defendant know the difference between right and wrong?" If, despite mental impairment the defendant knew he was shooting at a human being and intended murder, such a person could be held criminally responsible. Mental disease would provide a defense only if it prevented this defendant from realizing that he was firing a gun or made him believe he was shooting something other than a person. Psychiatric testimony delving into the defendant's toilet training, breast-feeding, childhood conflicts, and juvenile cronies would be precluded because of their disservice to an understanding of the defendant's mental state at the time of the crime. The focus of psychiatric testimony would be limited to the defendant's degree of awareness at the time of the offending act.

Objections could easily be raised against this proposal. It might seem that this proposal would liberalize the *mens rea* defense beyond its present boundaries and, furthermore, that it would create a broad defense of diminished capacity. The facts seem otherwise. In the first place, the *mens rea* insanity defense would not involve the subjective psychiatric histories characteristic of existing insanity trials, but would instead involve a narrower focus on the statutory definitions of mental state. In most jurisdictions these mental states are no longer broad concepts like "malice" or "moral turpitude," but narrowly defined psychological descriptions of discrete degrees of cognitive awareness. In effect, these narrow statutory definitions would constitute the only test for insanity. In response to the diminished capacity argument, the fact is that diminished capacity already exists in principle in any criminal code which either defines lesser included offenses (for instance, degrees of murder or of theft) or which adopts the Model Pean Code's hierarchy of the four mental states of intent, knowledge, recklessness, and negligence. These typical statutory schemes implicitly adopt a theory of diminished capacity because they recognize degrees of culpability based on degrees of insight. Thus, now, when defendants are convicted of lesser-included offenses, it is in virtue of these existing diminished capacity concepts rather than because of the insanity defense itself.

The consequences of such a modified abolition for the criminal justice system would be beneficial as well as constitutional. In the first place, the adoption of a consistent philosophy of criminal responsibility would enhance both the credibility and the deterrent message of the criminal justice system. The insanity defense would be rightly retained, as it must, but its patchwork medical formulations would yield to a more enduring, commonsense approach likely to be more intelligible to jurors, less seductive to pontificating psychiatrists, and more consistent with the common law prior to *M'Naghten*. Psychiatric histories and testimonials would reduce as evidence focuses more narrowly on whether the defendant had the capacity to act with the intent, awareness, or recklessness defined by statute. Insanity would revert to its proper role as a legal rather than medical issue. Finally, as the law adopts the medical view of insanity as a fluctuating rather than fixed state, there would be less likelihood that juries would face the all-or-nothing binary choice, as in Hinckley, of a first-degree murder conviction or total acquittal; convictions for some demented defendants could occur for lesser-included offenses, thereby acknowledging lesser guilt and also serving society's need for conviction.

6. Epilogue: A word on commitment

Any comprehensive response to the problems of the insanity defense must take into account the closely related problem of the civil commitment of the acquitted insane person.

It is clear that a jury's verdict of acquittal would not by itself provide a basis for institutionalization under the approach urged here. Yet even without a special verdict, there is a good reason why courts should act on evidence of illness by fashioning an appropriate civil commitment procedure.

Automatic commitment and commitment at the discretion of the trial judge are both subject to serious constitutional questions, principally due to the lack of the due process safeguards available under ordinary civil commitment. Automatic commitment is also subject to constitutional question insofar as it is based on a determination of the defendant's mental condition at the time of the act rather than at the time of the trial.

The civil commitment model offers a working model but only a partial one. That model requires a finding of a recent overt act of dangerousness as the prelude to authorizing commitment. It also usually sets a relatively short period for observation and review, typically a hundred eighty days. Often the civil commitment model provides for temporary passes and even outright release from the institution on the medical judgment of the institution's attending doctors.

While these ordinary procedures may be appropriate for non-criminal mentally ill persons, they fail to provide sufficient protection for the mentally ill showing criminal tendencies. What appears to be needed is a special commitment procedure for persons acquitted because of insanity. Such a system should provide for the possibility of long-term hospitalization, periodic review over a longer period than in civil cases, and court approval of hospital release. One of the most feasible approaches is to fashion civil commitment standards which use past criminal behavior as a rebuttable presumption of the dangerousness required for commitment. It may also be appropriate to shift the burden of persuasion to the defendant to show why commitment is inappropriate. Furthermore, legislatures should consider increasing the stringency of standards for the release of committed persons by requiring judicial review of psychiatrists' release orders. The major problem in this area consists of a patient's ability to act "normal" when given massive does of medication in an institution, which prompts psychiatrists to declare the person cured and releasable. Problems begin almost as soon as the released pateint discontinues medication. In many cases, these unmedicated individuals are walking time bombs ready to explode. This situaiton suggests that the judicial review of a medical recommendation for release should include some assurance both from the doctor and the patient of the patient's willingness and ability to continue to take prescribed medication.

Conclusion

The insanity defense constitutes a rallying ground for the increasing tension in the criminal law between competing concepts of personal responsibility and determinism. The defense's symbolic importance in eliciting this debate far exceeds its practical mechanics in those rare cases where it is invoked. This philosophical tension continues to increase, but a *modus vivendi* may reside in the recognition of the experiential basis for the postulate of freedom. In the criminal law that postulate resides in concepts other than any particular insanity "test." Neither of the two existing generic insanity defenses—the one based on *mens rea*, the other on a series of medical definitions—is needed to ground this postulate of freedom.

The elimination of the excuse function would undermine neither the freedom of will postulate nor the law's humane concern for the sick. If anything is undermined it would be the permissiveness and trickery perceived in the special verdict of acquittal. While the total exclusion of the insanity evidence from the courtroom is both inhumane and unconstitutional, consolidation of the special excuse function into the broader "element of the crime" defense would most likely reduce psychiatric case histories in court, recognize a more accurate concept of fluctuating degrees of insanity, and liberate legal insanity from passing psychiatric fads. In the process, the public's perception of the law's general deterrent purpose and its specific concepts of freedom and cognitive awareness would be enhanced.

FOOTNOTES

INTRODUCTION

1. The interest has increased since the acquittal of John Hinckley from the charge of attempted assassination of President Reagan.

2. The Federal Criminal Code (proposed), SB 1, (1975).

3. *Morris, The Honest Politician's Guide To Crime Control* (1972). See also his *Madness and the Criminal Law* (1982).

4. See generally *Freud, A General Introduction To Psychoanalysis* 93 (1935), where the author writes:

> I have already taken the liberty of pointing out to you that there is within you a deeply rooted belief in psychic freedom and choice, that this belief is quite unscientific, and that it must give ground before the claims of a determinism which governs even mental life.

5. One jurist articulated this view in these words:

> The law's conception, resting as it does upon an undemonstrable view of man, is of course vulnerable. But those who attack it cannot offer a view which is demonstrably more authentic. They can tear down the edifice but have nothing better to replace it.

State v. Sikora, 44 J.J. 453, 475, 210 A.2d 193, 205 (1965) (Weintraub, concurring). Chief Justice Weintraub appears to hold the view that psychiatry and criminal law operate on sets of separate and inconsistent assumptions. See State v. Lucas, 30 N.J. 37, 152 A.2d 50 (1959); Weintraub (Panel), *Insanity as a Defense*, 37 F.R.D. 365, 369-75 (1964).

6. *Id.*

7. See *Kalven, Empirical Inquiry and Legal Policy*, in *Law in a Changing America* 58 (Hazard, ed., 1968), and *Huckabee, Lawyers, Psychiatrists, and Criminal Law* (1980).

CHAPTER 1

1. Wigmore, *Responsibility for Tortious Acts*, 7 *Harv. Law Rev.* 317 (1894).

2. Mueller, *Tort, Crime, and the Primitive*, J. *Crim. Law, Criminology & Police Sci.*, 302 (1955).

3. "A deaf-mute, an idiot, and a minor are awkward to deal with, as he who injures them is liable [to pay], whereas if they injure others they are exempt." *The Babylonia Talmud, Baba Kamma* 501-2 (Epstein, ed., 1935), pp. 501-2.

> "To clash with a deaf mute, an imbecile, or a minor is bad, seeing that if one wounds one of these, he is liable, whereas if they wound others, they are exempt. Even if a deaf-mute becomes normal, or an imbecile becomes sane, or a minor reaches majority, they are not liable for payment inasmuch as they were legally irresponsible when they caused the wound.

Code of Maimon, The Book of Torts, Book Eleven, (Oberman, ed., 1954).

4. *Plato, Laws, Book IX*, 256 (Taylor, transl., 1931).

5. *Plato, The Republic* 350 (Cornford, transl., 1915). See also Agretelis, *Mens Rea in Plato and Aristotle, Issues in Criminology*, 19 (1969).

6. *Aristotle, The Nicomachean Ethics* 58 (Ross, transl., 1954).

> (I)f the acts that are in accordance with the virtues have themselves a certain character, it does not follow that they are done justly or temperately. The agent also must be in a certain condition when he does them; in the first place he must have knowledge, secondly he must choose the acts, and choose them for their own sakes, and thirdly his action must proceed from a firm and unchangeable character

Id. at 34. Aristotle also saw the ability to do otherwise as the hallmark of freedom: "For what lies in our power to do, lies in our power not to do." *Id., Book III*.

7. *Justinian, Digest*. 48.4.2

8. *The Venerable Bede, In Cantica Canticorum Allegorica Exposito*, lib. 1, 1070.

9. *Biggs, The Guilty Mind* 83 (1955).

10. Guttmacher attributes the "wild beast" test to Bracton. Guttmacher, *A Historical Outline of the Criminal Law's Attitude Toward Mental Disorder*, 4 *Archives Crim. Psychodynamics*, 688 (1971), as do *Glueck, Mental Disorder And The Criminal Law* 125-27 (1925), and *Biggs, The Guilty Mind* 82 (1955). But as clear in Platt,

The Origins and Development of the "Wild Beast" Concept of Mental Illness and its Relation to Theories of Criminal Responsibility, 1 *Issues In Criminology,* 1 (1965), Bracton's "wild beast" test was misinterpreted by English courts. Bracton used the Latin term *brutis* to mean brutes; that is, animals, who lack reason; he did not intend to associate the insane with wild beasts seized with diabolical possessions.

11. *Biggs, The Guilty Mind* 83 (1955). See also *Glueck, Mental Disorder And The Criminal Law* 125 (1925); Eliasberg, *Urge and Motivation in Criminology,* 43 *J. Crim. Law, Criminology & Police Sci.,* 319 (1952), and *Goldstein, The Insanity Defense* (1967).

12. *Id.*

13. Platt and Diamond, *The Origins and Development of the "Wild Beast" Concept of Mental Illness and its Relation to Theories of Criminal Responsibility,* 1 *J. Hist. Behavioral Sciences,* 355 (1965).

14. *Lambard, Eirenarchea, Or Of The Office Of Justices of Peace* 213 (1931).

15. *Coke, Institute of the Laws of England, or a Commentary Upon Littleton* 247 (11th ed., 1719).

16. *Hale, The History of the Pleas of the Crown* 25 (1736).

17. *Id.* at 30.

18. *Id.* at 30. The second class of disorders, *dementia accidentalis vel adventitia,* was further divided into two classes, partial insanity and total insanity. Partial insanity was distinguished from total insanity in that it was of a lesser degree or limited to "particular discourses, subjects, or applications." Hale believed that many suffering from partial insanity are not "wholy destitute of reason" and so are accountable for their capital crimes. They are to be distinguished, however, from those persons suffering from "perfect" insanity who have lucid intervals (that is, lunatics). These persons are not criminally liable for acts done during periods of insanity.

The wild beast test may be due to a misinterpretation of Bracton's "wild beast" test of insanity. Hale wrote: "...these dements are both in the same rank; if they are totally deprived of the use of reason, they cannot be guilty ordinarily of capital offenses, for they have not the use of understanding, and act not as reasonable creatures, but their actions are in the condition of brutes." *Hale, Historia Placitorum Coronae* 31-32 (1847). See also note 10 above.

19. *Hale, Pleas of the Crown* 14 (1945).

20. *Id.* 30.

21. *The Trial of Edward Arnold, How. State Trails,* 16 (1724), 695, 764-65. Mr. Justice Tracy aded that "...punishment is intended for example, and to deter other persons from wicked designs; but the punishment of a madman...can have no example."

22. In Regina v. Oxford, 173 Eng. Rep. 941 (C.P. 1840), Lord Chief Justice Denman makes reference to control and resistance. "If some controlling disease was, in truth, the acting power within him which he could not resist, then he will not be responsible." *Id.* at 950. It is a reasonable conclusion that if, following the *Oxford* case, the lords had asked the judges to state the test when insanity is set up as a defense they would have responded in the language employed by Lord Denman to the jury.

CHAPTER 2

1. This chapter is indebted to the research of *Biggs, The Guilty Mind* (1955), *Endler, Holiday of Darkness* (1982), and *Morris, Madness and the Criminal Law* (1982).

CHAPTER 3

1. 8 Eng. Rep. 718 (1843).

2. With some modification, the history of the *M'Naghten* Rule follows *The First Report of The Special Commission On Insanity and Criminal Offenders* (Calif.) 73 (July 7, 1962) (hereinafter cited *Commission Rep't*) addressed to the governor and legislature of California. The chairman of the Special Commission on Substantive Problems was Thomas C. Lynch, then district attorney of San Francisco County, who was succeeded in November 1960, by Arthur H. Sherry, Professor of Law and Criminology, University of California, Berkeley. This account also follows to some extent the excellent survey in Becker, *Durham Revisited,* 8-9 *Psychiatric Annals,* 3 (1973).

3. "We feel the evidence, especially that of the last two medical gentlemen who have been examined, and who are strangers to both sides and only observers of the case, to be very strong, and sufficient to induce my learned brother and myself to stop the case." The Queen v. Daniel M'Naghten, 4 State Trials, N.S., 847, 924 (1953).

4. *Id.* at p. 926.

5. For a discussion of the newspaper and other attacks, see *Biggs, The Guilty Mind* 102 (1955).

6. quoted in *Glueck, Mental Disorder and the Criminal Law* 164 (1927).

7. Ellison and Haas, *A Recent Judicial Interpretation of the M'Naghten Rule,* 4 Brit. J. Delinquency 129 (1953), as quoted in Roche, *Criminality and Mental Illness—Two Faces of the Same Coin,* 22 U. Chi. L. Rev. 320, 324 (1955).

8. The Queen v. Daniel M'Naghten, 4 State Trials, N.S., 847, 930-52 (1843).

9. *Biggs, The Guilty Mind* 107 (1955). In a later edition of his book Dr. Isaac Ray commented adversely on *M'Naghten's* formulations. See *Ray, A Treatise On The Medical Jurisprudence Of Insanity* 39 (4th ed., 1860). For an early discussion of the legal origins and attendant confusions in Tindal's answers, see *Glueck, Mental Disorder And The Criminal Law* 161-86 (1925). There seems little doubt that the *M'Naghten* formulation embodied intellectualistic psychology. Delusional insanity seems to have been the chief if not the only kind of insanity the judges had in mind, since their view was that insanity was a defect in the intellectual-perceptual faculties. The test arose from a case involving delusion and at a time when delusion was sine qua non of insanity. Cf. *Fingarette, The Meaning of Criminal Insanity* 239 (1972).

10. *Goldstein, The Insanity Defense* 45 (1967). For the historical background of *M'Naghten,* see Wingo, *Squaring M'Naghten with Precedent—An Historical Note,* 26 S. C. L. Rev. 81 (1974).

CHAPTER 4

1. Cf. 21 Am. Jur. 2d Sec. 33 (1965) and Blocker v. United States, 320 F. 2d 800 (D.C. Cir. 1963).

2. See *Simon, The Jury and the Defense of Insanity* (1967), for history. Some courts have denied any distinction between the two different branches of the test. The reason given for disregarding the difference usually is that "if the accused did not know the nature and quality of his act, he would have been incapable of knowing it was wrong." This reasoning assumes that an accused must know the nature and quality of his act before he can know whether his act was wrong. In fact there is a necessary and logical connection between *M'Nagten's* two branches. One presumes the other.

This does not mean, however, that the *M'Naghten* Test is satisfied by showing that the defendant knew that he was doing wrong. The prosecutor must establish both conditions—that the accused knew the nature and quality of his act and that he knew that the act was wrong. The defendant thus has two exculpatory strings to his bow.

It is a mistake, therefore, to treat the different arms of the test synonymously and to give instructions relating to only one branch, or to interpret *M'Naghten* in the conjunctive to require an accused to satisfy both branches before qualifying for the de-fense. Such a conjunctive treatment of *M'Naghten* may be a reversible error. A person might know the nature and quality of his act but not know that it is wrong. Conversely, a man might say that he knew his act was wrong, but he may not have appreciat-ed its nature and quality. Occasional examples illustrate the difference. A defendant knew the nature and quality of his act when he chloroformed his sixteen-year-old son, a congenital imbecile, but believed his act to be "right" because he was commanded by the "will of God." In another case the defendant knew the nature of his act but believed "that he had heard the voice of God calling upon him to kill the victim as a sacrifice and atonement."

3. "*Mens rea* accordingly was a sense of wrongdoing, an appreciation of the wrongfulness of the act. Thus, the capacity to commit a crime was at common law the capacity to see right from wrong." Weintraub, *Criminal Responsibility: Psychiatry Alone Cannot Determine it,* 49 A.B.A.J., 1076 (1963).

4. Comment, *Criminal Responsibility and Insanity: Past—Pres-ent—Future,* 27 Tenn. L. Rev., 389, 395 (1960). "[W]e should ask for evidence and a great deal of evidence before we accept the irrationalism that one's reason may be unimpaired and that nonetheless it exercises no control over such conduct." Hall, *Mental Disease and Criminal Responsibility—M'Naghten Versus Durham and the American Law Institute's Tentative Draft,* 33 Ind. L.J., 212-14 (1958).

5. See Hall, *Mental Disease and Criminal Responsibility— M'Naghten Versus Durham and the American Law Institute's Tentative Draft,"* 33 Ind. L.J. 212 (1958). Hall, *Responsibility and Law: In Defense of the M'Naghten Rules,"* 42 A.B.A.J., 917 (1956); Goldstein, *The Insanity Defense* 49 (1967).

6. See Goldstein, supra, note 5 at 45.

7. See Weihoffen, *Definition of Mental Illness,* 2 Ohio St. L.J., 1 (1960).

8. Zilbourg, *Misconceptions of Legal Insanity*, 22 *U. Chi. L. Rev.* 331 (195).

9. *Amer. J. Orthopsychiatry*, 540-53 (1939). Zilbourg does not blame the law, but holds that "the incongruity is caused by lack of clarity as to standards within the medical profession itself." *Id.* at p. 553.

> The extreme cases of such divorcement between purely intellectual or verbal perception and full realistic perception present a clear-cut schizophrenic picture. But not only the fully developed schizophrenic is afflicted with such a split between word-concept and fact. We know that such compulsion neurotics, or obsessional neurotics, manifest the same clinical phenomenon, which in these cases is called isolation ...(T)he obsessional thought or the compulsive act is isolated effectively from the rest of the personality and becomes nonintegrated knowledge, or no knowledge at all.

It seems well recognized that the word *know* in the *M'Naghten* Test should mean more than purely intellectual understanding. Professor Hall, Dr. Zilbourg, and Professors Fingarette and Mueller all assert that the term properly means "to appreciate" or "to understand." Cf. *Fingarette, The Meaning of Criminal Insanity* 147 (1972).

10. *Report of the Royal Commission on Capital Punishment* (1953).

11. Roche, *Criminal Responsibility and Mental Disease: Medical Aspects*, 26 *Tenn. L. Rev.* 222 (1959); Roche, *Criminality and Mental Illness—Two Faces of the Same Coin*, 22 *U. Chi. L. Rev.* 320, 321 (1954-55).

12. Zilboorg, *supra* note 8.

13. Diamond, *Criminal Responsibility of the Mentally Ill*, 14 *Stan. L. Rev.* 59 (1961).

14. Dr. Diamond has stated the issue:

> Whenever a psychiatrist is called upon to testify, under the *M'Naghten* Rule...the psychiatrist must either renounce his own values with all their medical-humanistic implications, thereby becoming a puppet doctor, used by the law to further the punitive and vengeful goals demanded by our society; or he must commit perjury if he accepts a literal definition of the *M'Naghten* Rule. If he tells the truth—stating ...that just about every defendant, no matter how mentally ill, no matter how far advanced his psychosis, knows the difference between right and wrong...he becomes an expeditor to the gallows or gas chamber."

Diamond, *Criminal Responsibility of the Mentally Ill,* 14 *Stan. L. Rev.,* 59-61 (1961).

CHAPTER 5

1. State v. Thompson, Wright's Ohio Rep. 617 (1834). See also Clark v. State, 12 Ohio Rep. 483 (1843).

2. See State v. Smith, 223 Kan. 203, 574 P 2d 548 (1977) for a list of the states.

3. State v. White, 58 N.M. 324, 270 P.2d 727, 731 (1954). Cf. also Parsons v. State, 81 Ala. 577, 2 So. 834 (1887).

4. *Goldstein, The Insanity Defense* 69 (1967).

5. In Snider v. Smyth, 187 F. Supp. 299, 302 (E.D. Va. 1960), aff'd 282 F.2d 683 (4th Cir. 1961), the jury was told that if the defendant had planned his act, he could not come within the irresistible-impulse test, and to come within it, the defendant's act had to be of the type that "comes upon a person rather hurriedly; it rises quickly; short of interference by a third party, it is irresistible." In De Jarnette v. Commonwealth, 75 Va. 867 (1881), discussed in Thompson v. Commonwealth, 193 Va. 704, S.E. 2d 284, 292 (1952), the court rested heavily on the notion of suddenness, requiring that the defendant's mental disease "break out in a sudden paroxysm of violence."

6. Goldstein, *supra,* note 4 at 70-75 and *Hall, Psychiatry and Criminal Responsibility* (1956), at 76-78, claim that the presentation of evidence, in fact, is not greatly restricted, but the possibility still remains under the narrowly worded tests.

7. E.g., People v. Sherwood, 271 N.Y. 427, 3 N.E. 2d 281 (1936).

8. *Guttmacher, The Role of Psychiatry in Law* 51 (1968). Numerous acts result from "uncontrollable compulsions, many of [which] have a sexual basis. The most serious of these is arson." *Id.* at p. 42; see also Durham v. United States, 214 F.2d 862, 872-74 (D.C. Cir. 1954).

9. Goldstein suggests that there is no such "irresistible-impulse" test per se, and that it is just a "text writer's caption" which most cases do not even use, and that it really means a "control test." Goldstein, *supra,* note 4 at 69.

10. *Id.*

CHAPTER 6

1. Durham v. United States, 94 U.S. App. D.C. 228, 214 F.2d 862 (1954).

2. See United States v. Lee, 15 D.C. 489, 496, 4 Mackey 489, 496 (1886) ("right-wrong" test); Smith v. United States, 59 App. D.C. 144, 36 F.2d 548 (1929) (adding "irresistible impulse" to the test).

3. Durham v. United States, 94 U.S. App. D.C. 228, 240, 241, 214 F.2d 862, 874, 875 (1954). The major problems with the right-wrong test were analyzed in detail by the *Durham* court. That test failed to recognize that "a man is an integrated personality and that reason (cognition), which is only one element in that personality, is not the sole determinant of his conduct." 214 F2d at 871. Furthermore, the irresistible impulse supplement to *M'Naghten* was found to be too narrow since it did not recognize that all volitional impairment need not be impulsive.

For a more complete analysis of the defects in such a restricted volitional test, see Wade v. United States, 426 F2d 64, 67 (9th Cir. 1970); United States v. Freeman, 357 F.2d 606, 620-21 (2d Cir. 1966); Carter v. United States, 252, F2d 608, 616 (D.C. Cir. 1957); Model Penal Code § 4.01, Comment at 157 (Tent. Draft No. 4, 1955).

4. Kalven, *Insanity and the Criminal Law—A Critique of Durham v. United States: Introduction,* 22 *Chi. L. Rev.* 317, 318 (1954-55).

5. Letter from Judge Hand to editors of the University of Chicago Law Review, 22 *U. Chi. L. Rev.* 319 (1954-55).

6. Szasz, *Psychiatry, Ethics, and the Criminal Law,* 58 *Colum. L. Rev.* 183, 190 (1958).

7. Zilboorg, *A Step Toward Enlightened Justice,* 22 *U. Chi. L. Rev.* 331, 335 (1954-55).

8. Kalven, *supra,* note 4 at 318.

9. Central to the difficulties with any definition of legal insanity is the all-or-none conceptualization of the law. A defendant is either sane and totally responsible, or insane and not at all responsible. Such all-or-none concepts are peculiarly foreign to modern psychiatric thinking. Neither normal persons nor mentally disturbed persons are ever "all-or-none" in their psychological functioning. When such an arbitrary division is required of the psychiatrist-expert, he is liable to testify capriciously and not in accord with all of the psychological facts of the case.
Diamond, *Criminal Responsibilsity of the Mentally Ill,* 14 *Stan. L. Rev.* 59, 62 (1961), See also Model Penal Code § 4.01, Comment at 157-58 (Tent. Draft No. 4, 1955).

10. Hospers, *Free-Will and Psychoanalysis,* in *Readings in Ethical Theory* 571-75 (1952). (Emphasis added) See also Louisell and Diamond, *Law and Psychiatry: Detente, Entente, or Concomitance* 50 *Corn. L.Q.,* 217 (1965).

11. Reid, *The Bell Tolls for Durham,* 6 *J. Offender Therapy,* 58 (1962).

TABLE A

**Persons Found Not Guilty by Reason of Insanity
(U.S. District Court for the District of Columbia,
fiscal years 1954-1966)**

Fiscal Year	Defendants in Cases Terminated[1]	Defendants in Cases Tried[1]	Defendants NGI[2]	NGI as Percent of Defendants in Cases Terminated	NGI as Percent of Defendants in Cases Tried
1954[3]	1,870	673	3	0.2	0.4
1955	1,384	453	8	.6	1.8
1956	1,595	456	16	1.0	3.5
1957	1,454	456	7	.5	1.5
1958	1,666	522	17	1.0	3.3
1959	1,642	528	32	1.9	6.1
1960	1,367	400	35	2.6	8.8
1961	1,337	457	66	4.9	14.4
1962	1,282	480	66	5.1	13.8
1963	1,183	398	53	4.5	13.3
1964	1,142	393	23	2.0	5.9
1965	1,286	372	35	2.7	9.4
1966	1,230	380	26	2.1	6.8
Total	18,438	5,968	387	2.1	6.5

[1]Source: Administrative Office of the United States Courts. [Abstracted from President's Commission on Crime in the District of Columbia, Report 535 (1966)—ed.]

[2]"NGI"—not guilty by reason of insanity in this and subsequent tables.

[3]The fiscal year preceding the decision in *Durham v. United States.* Prior to this year, insanity patients were not recorded separately from all other prisoner patients at Saint Elizabeth's Hospital.

Source of Table: Arens, The Insanity Defense 17 (1974).

12. *Arens, The Insanity Defense* (1974).

13. *Id.*

14. Blocker v. United States, 288 F.2d 859, 860-61 (1961). also Campbell v. United States, 307 Fed. 597.

15. Frigillana v. United States, 307 F.2d 670 (1962).

16. 343 F.2d 272 (1964).

17. Bleechmore, *The Denial of Responsibility as a General Defense,* 23 *Ala. L. Rev.* 237, 249 (1971).

18. M. R. S. A. Tit. 15, Sec. 102 (1964); Virgin Is. Code, Tit. 14, Sec. 14 (4) (1964).

CHAPTER 7

1. United States v. Brawner, 471 F.2d 969 (D.C. Cir. 1972).

2. Model Penal Code, § 4.01 (Tent. Draft No. 4, 1955).

3. Brawner, 471 F.2d at 992. See Platt, *Choosing a Test for Criminal Insanity*, 5 *Willamette, L.J.*, 553 (1969).

4. Brawner, 471 F.2d at 992.

5. *Id.* at p. 993. The caveat paragraph has only been rejected by two circuits which have adopted the substance of the ALI Rule. See Wade v. United States, 426 F.2d 64, 72 (9th Cir. 1970); United States v. Smith, 404 F.2d 720, 727 n.8 (6th Cir. 1968).

6. Brawner, 471 F.2d at 986.

7. The British Royal Commission on Capital Punishment proposed:

> [A person is not responsible for his unlawful act if] at the time of the act [he] was suffering from such a disease of the mind [or mental deficiency] to such a degree that he ought not to be held responsible.

Report of the Royal Commission on Capital Punishment 1949-53, § 333 (iii) (1953).

A minority of the ALI Council, including Professor Wechsler, proposed a similar insanity test which reads:

> A person is not responsible for criminal conduct if at the time of such conduct as a result of mental disease or defect his capacity either to appreciate the criminality of his conduct or to conform his conduct to the requirements of law is so substantially impaired that he cannot justly be held responsible.

Model Penal Code § 4.01, Alternative (a) to paragraph (1) (Tent. Draft No. 4, 1955).

Chief Judge Bazelon's proposed rule is still another variation of the "justly responsible" rule. See Brawner at 1022 (concurring opinion); United States v. Eichberg, 439 F.2d 620, 625 (D.C. Cir. 1971) (concurring opinion).

8. Brawner, 471 F.2d at 1022. Professor Goldstein also concludes that juries would find it easier to perform their assigned role if they know that their verdicts are "required" by law, *Goldstein, The Insanity Defense*, at 73.

9. Brawner, 471 F.2d at 1008. (Appendix B: Suggestion for Instruction on Insanity)

10. *Id.* at p. 985-86.

11. Confusion between *mens rea* and insanity is widespread. Burger, then judge in the Appellate Court, District of Columbia,

said in 1962 in connection with the question of insanity and criminal responsibility:

> I will conclude by saying that the precise words of any formulation on criminal responsibility are not particularly important. The important thing that we must remember is that *mens rea*, "criminal intent," is the center of it. That is the inquiry the law is making, and any test or any formulation is adequate if it is based upon the concept of cognition, that is, recognition of the nature of the act and its wrongness, and volition or capacity to control conduct. If the standard has those elements the particular words are not important. If it doesn't have those elements, it breaks continuity with all of the law of the past"

(Proceed. 10th Cir., 1962, p. 564).

Burger here explicitly associates insanity with the questions of knowledge and volition. A reference to insanity that explicitly puts an emphasis on *mens rea* rather than any other issues is that of Chief Justice Weintraub (1964) in his remarks to the 2nd Circuit Judicial Conference Symposium on "Insanity as a Defense":

> If because of mental illness a man could not tell right from wrong, he lacked capacity to commit crime. In other words, the mental illness met head-on the state's charge that the evil act is done with an evil mind. And although we some-times speak of insanity as a defense, it is not a separate defense, as we lawyers use that concept, to a case that the state has otherwise established but, rather, it is essentially a denial of the state's main case, a denial of *mens rea*

(p. 370). Professor Wechsler in his comments at the same symposium remarks that "the criterion of responsibility as affected by disease or defect parallels the traditional *mens rea* rules in requiring a determination of blameworthiness in the ordinary moral sense" (p. 381). Judge Biggs also in effect criticizes the *Durham* formula because in it there is no explanation of how that formula "expresses a relationship between mental disease and guilty mind, or *mens rea*" (Proceed. 10th Cir., 1962, p. 551).

12. Brawner, 471 F.2d at 1012. *Arens, The Insanity Defense* (1974) argues more stridently that the replacement of *Durham* by *Brawner* has not significantly improved the insanity test, which, according to Lasswell's foreward (p. xxiv), is still inspired by *M'Naghten's* cognitive, free-will doctrine, whatever words are used.

13. *Fingarette, The Meaning of Criminal Insanity* 242 (1972).

14. Wechsler, *Codification of the Criminal Law in the United*

States: The Moral Penal Code, 68 *Colum. L. Rev.* 1425, 1443 (1968).
15. Fingarette, *supra,* note 13 at 242-3.
16. *Id.*
17. *Biggs, The Guilty Mind* 60 (1955).
18. Model Penal Code, Sec. 4.01, comments at 160.
19. Biggs, *supra,* note 17 at 160.
20. Kozol, *The Psychopath Before the Law,* 44 *Mass. L.Q.* 106, 116 (No. 2, July 1959).
21. The German provision is found at StGB 1871, Secs. 51 and 20; The Soviet is at Ugol. kod (RSFSR), sec. 11.
22. *Brawner* requires a "mental disease or defect." StGB sec 20 lists the following specific conditions: "a diseased mental disturbance, a deep disturbance to consciousness, weak-mindedness, or a serious mental defect." The Soviet test requires "a chronic mental illness, a temporary disturbance of mental activity, weak-mindedness, or any other diseased condition."
23. The comparable German provision in StGB sec. 20 requires that the actor be incapable of acting according to his perception" that the conduct is wrong. The Soviet provision requires that the actor "not be able to control his action." *Id.*

CHAPTER 8

1. This discussion relies in part on the analysis given in Comment, *Mens Rea and Insanity,* 28 *Me. L. Rev.* 500 (1976), beginning at page 506. There are significant differences with some of the conclusions drawn in that analysis. The statute involved is Me. Rev. St. An. 17-A § 59 (1976).
2. 4 *Blackstone, Commentaries* 21 (Lewis ed., 1898).
3. See Kadish, *The Decline of Innocence,* 26 *Camb. L.J.* 273 (1968).
4. See Overholsen v. Lynch, 288 F. 2d 388, 393 (D.C. Cir. 1961), rev'd on other grounds, 369 U.S. 705.
5. 160 U.S. 469 (1895).
6. *Blackstone, Commentaries* 21 (Lewis ed., 1898).
7. Davis v. U.S., *supra,* note 5 at 485. *In re Winship,* 397 U.S. 358, 364 (1970).
8. 290 F.2d 751 (3d Cir. 1961).
9. See note 1, *supra.*
10. Leache v. State, 3 S.W. 539, 22 Tex. App. 279 (1886).
11. 421 U.S. 684 (1975).
12. 343 U.S. 790 (1952).

13. 421 U.S. at 706 (Rehnquist concurring.)

14. See Note 1 *supra*, at 529.

15. Fingarette, *Insanity*, 76 *Colum. L. Rev.* 236 (1976).

16. The Royal Commission on Capital Punishment (1953) observed that a criminal act could be "coolly and carefully prepared" and still be the "act of a madman." *Id.* at 110. The commission suggested that this result would be consistent with mental states such as schizophrenia and paranoid psychoses.

CHAPTER 9

1. *Wootten, Crime and the Criminal Law* (1963).

2. Menninger, *Medico-Legal Proposals of the American Psychiatric Association*, 19 *J. Crim. Law, Criminology & Police Sci.*, 367-73 (1928). Lately Menninger has tempered his view to the confusing point where he now says that crime "is not an illness, although I think it should be," *The Crime of Punishment* 254 (1968).

3. Gaylin, *Psychiatry and the Law: Partners in Crime*, 8 *Colum. U. Forum* 23 (1965).

4. Wootten, *supra*, note 1, chapter 3 (1963).

5. *Packer, The Limits of the Criminal Sanction* (1969). Cf. also his *Enemies of Progress, N.Y. Rev. Books*, Oct. 23, 1969, p.17.

6. Much of this discussion is indebted to *Hart, Punishment and Responsibility* (1968). Wootten's major point is that we have no scientific way of "getting inside another's mind." Hart's response is simply that we accurately understand another's intention and purpose by such things as bodily movement and facial expressions.

7. "It is the environment which is responsible for the objectionable behavior, and it is the environment, not some attribute of the individual, that must be changed...[Our goal is] a better environment, not better men." *Skinner, Beyond Freedom and Dignity* 70,77 (1971).

8. Even if free will is an illusion, it is such a vital one that the law, as everyday life, must adopt it. See Kadish, *The Decline of Innocence*, 26 *Cambridge L.J.*, 273-88 (1968). The essential distinction between free choice and involuntary acts does not in fact necessitate a metaphysical doctrine of free will. If free will is unproven, or even if it is an illusion, it is such a commonplace and well-founded one that the law would be out of step with human experience to abandon it. Note, however, that modern codes do not express the concept of free will in *mens rea* but in the

requirement of a "voluntary act." See Model Penal Code, § 2.02.

9. United States v. Brawner, 471 F.2d 969, 985 (D.C. Cir. 1972).

CHAPTER 10

1. This section is partly indebted to parallel research by Professors Robinson and Fletcher. See Robinson, *Criminal Law Defenses: A Systematic Analysis*, 82 *Columbia L. Rev.* 199 (1982) and *Fletcher, Rethinking Criminal Law* (1978).

2. *Id.* See also *Packer, The Criminal Sanction* (1968).

3. Quoted by Attorney General Smith in Smith, *Limiting Insanity* 47 *Mo. L. Rev.* 610 (1982).

4. Robinson, *supra,* note 1 at 208.

CHAPTER 11

1. See Smith. *Limiting Insanity, 47 Mo. L. Rev.* 610 (1982).

2. See discussion in Comment, 31 *Emory L.J.* at 18 and 442 (1982). The applicable statute is Me. Rev. Stat. Ann. 17-1 § 59 (1976).

3. State v. Shaw, 106 Ariz. 103, 471 P.2d 715 (1970), cert. denied, 400 U.S. 1009 (1971); State ex rel. Boyd v. Green, 355 So. 2d 789 (Fla. 1978); Sanchez v. State, 567 P.2d (Wyo. 1977). In *Shaw,* the Arizona Supreme Court became the first court to hold explicitly that a bifurcation statute unconstitutionally denied criminal defendants due process because it excluded evidence of mental condition as a defense to the prosecution's assertion of intent during the guilt trial.

4. Comment, 31 *Emory L.J.* 442-43 (1982).

5. People v. Wells, 33 Cal. 2d at 360-61, 202 P2d at 72 (1949).

6. Mich. Comp. Laws § 768.36 (3) [Mich. Stat. Ann. § 28.1059 (3) (Callaghan 1978)]. Treatment may be provided by either the department of corrections or by the department of mental health. Id. Indiana amended its criminal procedure code in 1980 to permit a finding of GBMI if a defendant asserts the insanity defense. Pub. L. No. 204, § 1, 1980 Ind. Acts 1650. (currently codified at Ind. Code Ann. § 35-5-2-3) (Burns Supp. 1981) (repealed effective Sept. 1, 1982 by Pub. L. No. 928, § 9, 1981 Ind. Acts) (recodified at Ind. Code Ann. § 35-36-2-3) [Burns Supp. 1981) (effective Sept. 1, 1982)].

Illinois amended its criminal procedure code in 1981 to permit a finding of GBMI. Pub. Act No. 82-553, § 2, 1981 Ill. Legis. Serv. 2462 (West).

See Pub. Act No. 82-553, § 3, 1981 Ill. Legis. Serv. 2462 (West); Ind. Code Ann. § 35-5-2-6 (Burns Supp. 1981) (repealed effective Sept. 1, 1982 by Pub. L. No. 298, § 9, 1981 Ind. Acts) {recodified at Ind. Code Ann. § 35-36-2-5 (Burns Supp. 1981)}. Under the Illinois provision, a sentencing court has the discretion to order a defendant found GBMI to receive a mental examination before he is transferred to the Department of Corrections. Once he is transferred, however, the department must cause periodic inquiry and examination to be made concerning his mental illness and provide such treatment as it determines necessary. See Pub. Act No. 82-553, § 3, 1981 Ill. Legisl. Serv. 2462; Ill. Ann. Stat. ch. 38, §§ 1005-3-1, -2 (Smith-Hurd Supp. 1981).

Under the Indiana statute, "mentally ill" is defined as "having a psychiatric disorder which substantially disturbs a person's thinking, feeling, or behavior and impairs the person's ability to function" (including mental retardation). Ind. Code Ann. § 35-5-2-3 (c) (Burns Supp. 1981) (repealted effective Sept. 1, 1982 by Pub. L. No. 298, § 9, 1981 Ind. Acts) {recodified at Ind. Code Ann. § 35-36-1-1 (Burns Supp. 1981)}. The Illinois statute provides that:

> "(M)ental illness" or "mentally ill" means a substantial disorder of thought, mood, or behavior which afflicted a person at the time of the commission of the offense and which impaired that person's judgment, but not to the extent that he is unable to appreciate the wrongfulness of his behavior or is unable to conform his conduct to the requirements of law.

Judge W. Beasley of the Michigan Court of Appeals has observed that the Michigan statute may be unconstitutional for failing to provide promised treatments. See *Beasley, Michigan's GBMI Verdict,* 62 *Mich. Bar Journal* 204 (March, 1983).

7. In United States v. Trapnell, 495 F.2d 22 (2d Cir.), cert. denied, 419 U.S. 851 (1974), the court admitted evidence that Trapnell, while a patient at a hospital, had counseled a fellow patient, Padilla, about how to feign insanity. Padilla attributed his success to Trapnell's teachings on the art of acting insane. Trapnell was arrested at least twenty times for major crimes but served less than two years in jail. He claimed that he could "fool psychiatrists and psychologists in Florida, Texas, Maryland, New York, California, and Canada into believing that he was a genuine 'Dr. Jekyll and Mr. Hyde' normally a sane, honest man, whose mind, every so often was taken over by a sinister alter ego called 'Greg Ross.'" For the complete story of Trapnell, see *ASINOF, THE FOX IS CRAZY TOO: THE TRUE STORY OF GARRETT TRAPNELL, AD-*

VENTURER, SKYJACKER, BANK ROBBER, CON MAN, LOVER (1976).

8. Section 502 of the administration's proposed federal criminal code stated: "It is a defense to a prosecution under any federal statute that the defendant, as a result of mental disease or defect, lacked the state of mind required as an element of the offense charged. Mental disease or defect does not otherwise constitute a defense."

9. See, e.g., United States v. Hinckley, Crim. No. 81-306 (.D.D.C. June 21, 1982).

10. See Goldstein and Katz, *Abolish the Insanity Defense—Why Not?* 72 *YALE L.J.* 853, 854-57 (1963); Robinson, *Criminal Law Defenses: A Systematic Analysis,* 82 *COLUM. L. REV.* 199, 213-16 (1982). See also Chapter 5, *supra, passim.*

11. See, e.g. Smith, *Limiting Insanity,* 47 *Mo. L. Rev.* 610 (1982).

12. Shawyer and Kurdys, *Less Insanity in the Courts,* 68 *A.B.A.J.* 824 (1982); Morris, *Psychiatry and the Dangerous Criminal,* 41 *S. CAL. L. REV.* 514 (1968).

13. *Rocoeur, La Volontaire et L'Involontaire* (1950) and *La Symbolique du Mal* (1960).

14. *Packer, The Limits of the Criminal Sanction* 133 (1968). Goldstein and Katz, *Abolish the Insanity Defense—Why Not?* 72 *Yale L.J.* 853 (1963).

15. 357 F.2d 606 (2d Cir. 1966). See also Robitscher, *In Defense of the Insanity Defense,* 31 *Emory L.J.* 9 (1982), to which this analysis is indebted.

16. State v. Strasberg, 60 Wash. 106, 110 p. 1020 (1910).

17. State v. Strasberg, *supra,* note 16, and Sinclair v. State, 161 Miss. 142, 132 So. 581 (1931).

18. Sinclair v. State, *supra,* 132 So. at 584.

19. State v. Strasberg, *supra,* note 17 at 1023.

20. State v. Sinclair, *supra,* note 18 at 584.

21. *Id.* at 584.

22. Spring, *The End of Insanity,* 19 *Wash. L. J.* 23, 33 (1979).

23. See the helpful discussion in Spring, *supra,* note 22 and section 46-14-101 of the Montana Criminal Code.

24. See Sec. 502 of the original federal criminal code bill, S.1 (1973).

25. State v. Strasberg, 60 Wash. 106, 110P 1020 (1910).

26. Sinclair v. State, 161 Miss. 142, 132 So. 581 (1931).

27. State v. Lange 168 La 958, 123 So. 639 (1929).

28. See the discussion of bifurcation, *supra,* in this chapter.

INDEX

Actus reus, 7
Affirmative defense
Alvarez, Bernadino, 13
American Law Institute test, 49, 50
Aristotle, 8, 18, 46
Arens, R., 45
Arnold's case, 11
Asylums, 18

Barrigan, Daniel, 68
Bazelon, D., 41, 42, 45-46
Beccaria, 19
Bedlam, 16, 23
Bentham, J., 18
Bicetre, 15, 16
Bifurcated trial, 78
Biggs, J., 53
Blackstone, 56
Blocker, 45
Bodin, J., 14
Boerhaave, H., 15
Bracton, H., 9, 25, 63
Brawner, 49-54
Burger, W., 45, 46, 47

Cartesian influence, 30
Cheyne, G., 15
Children, 10
Classifications of illness, 14, 15

Cognition test, 30, 32, 34, 37, 39
Coke, 10
Cullen, W., 15

Davis v. United States, 56
Defenses, 72
De Legibus et consuetudinibus Angliae, 9
Delusions, 26
Dementia, 19, 22
Diminished capacity, 73, 88
Disease of mind, 31
Dooms of Alfred, 8
Drummond, R., 21
Duality of mind and body, 7
Duress, 73
Durham test, 41-48

Erskine, L., 12
Esquirol, J., 16
Ethridge, J., 84
Evil v. sick mind, 48
Excuse, 72-73, 74, 86-87
Experts, 32

Ferrus, G., 16
Fingarette, H., 52, 60
Foucault, M., 41
Free will, 60, 68
Freedom, 8
Freud, S., 30
Furor, 19

Gaylin, W., 64
German Code, 53-54
Gheel, Belgium, 13
Goldstein, A., 30, 34, 39
Guilty but mentally ill, 79

Hadfield's Case, 12
Hale, 10, 11
Hall, J., 53
Hand, L. 42
Hebrew, 8
Hinckley, J., 12, 81, 85
Hospital of San Hipolito, 13

Illustrated London News, 23
Impulses, 39
In re Winship, 57
Irresistible impulse test, 37

Jung, C., 30
Justinian, 8

Kaufman, I., 83
King, Martin Luther, 68
King's grace, 9
Kolb, L., 33

La Salpetriere, 15
Lambard, 10
Legal realism, 64
Leprosariums, 14
Leslie v. Oregon, 59
Liberal treatment of insane, 16, 17
Loss of control, 39

Mansfield, C.J., 23
Maudslay, 26
Maule, J., 26
Medical Jurisprudence of Insanity, 21
Melancholia, 15, 38
Menninger, K., 41, 64
Mens reus, 7, 51, 55-61, 63
Mental degeneration, 27
M'Naghten, 11, 17, 21-27, 29-35

Model Penal Code, 53, 55, 58, 85, 88
Monomania, 26, 27, 30
Morgagni, G., 15
Moronic, 40
Mueller, G., 7, 8
Mullaney v. Wilbur, 58

Napoleonic laws, 19
Narrenschift, 14
New Hampshire, 29
Nixon, R., 81, 85

Onslow, 11

Packer, H., 66, 71
Paranoia, 38
Pardon, 9
Parsons v. State, 38
Peel, R., 21, 23
Philippe, L., 16
Phrenology, 11, 17, 18, 26
Pinel, P., 15
Plato, 8
Policy Presumption, 58
Poor laws, 17
Product test, 46
Pussin, J., 16

Ray, I., 21, 22, 25, 26
Reality principle, 31
Rehnquist, W., 58
Reid, Prof., 44
Responsibility, 35, 38, 43
Ricoeur, P., 82
Right-wrong test, 30, 38
Robinson, P., 72
Rogers, C., 30
Rollerson v. United States, 46
Royal Commission on Capital Punishment, 31

Rush, B., 17

Saint Elizabeth's Hospital, 44, 45
Saint Mary of Bethlehem, 13, 16
Saint Valentine's Hospital, 13
Scotland, 29
Sinclair v. State, 84
Skinner, B., 30, 68
Social defense, 64
Social deviancy, 68
Smith, W.F., 77-78
State v. Strasburg, 84
Stephen, J., 26
Strict liability, 69

Tindal, C.J., 22, 24, 26
Tory government, 24
Tracy, 10, 11
Truelock, B., 12
Turner, Prof., 63

United States v. Brawner, 49-54
United States v. Currens, 57
United States v. Freeman, 82
USSR Code, 53-54

Venerable Bede, 8
Victoria, Queen, 23
Volition, 39

Wade v. United States, 52
Walker, N., 30
Weyer, J., 13, 14
Whytt, R., 15
Wigmore, J., 7
Wild beast test, 9
Wingo, H., 25
Witchcraft, 13, 16, 18

Wootton, B., 64, 65, 68

XYZ chromosome, 68

Zilboorg, G., 29